THE ESSENTIALS OF
PARLIAMENTARY DEMOCRACY

MACMILLAN AND CO., Limited
LONDON · BOMBAY · CALCUTTA · MADRAS
MELBOURNE

THE MACMILLAN COMPANY
NEW YORK · BOSTON · CHICAGO
DALLAS · ATLANTA · SAN FRANCISCO

THE MACMILLAN COMPANY
OF CANADA, LIMITED
TORONTO

THE ESSENTIALS
OF
PARLIAMENTARY
DEMOCRACY

BY

R. BASSETT, B.A.

MACMILLAN AND CO., LIMITED
ST. MARTIN'S STREET, LONDON
1935

COPYRIGHT

PRINTED IN GREAT BRITAIN

To
MY MOTHER

The characteristic danger of great nations, like the Romans or the English, which have a long history of continuous creation, is that they may at last fail from not comprehending the great institutions which they have created.

WALTER BAGEHOT.

The chief argument for parliamentary government is that results are obtained by discussion between the divergent interests, and are imposed by consent—a method which produces a better average of humanity than the most scientific of despotisms.

PROFESSOR A. F. POLLARD.

INTRODUCTION

THIS book has been provoked by recent tendencies in British politics and by current controversies relative to the present working and future prospects of our system of parliamentary government. Its object is to elucidate or to re-state the conditions essential to the maintenance of parliamentary democracy. I have sought to explain what parliamentary democracy involves rather than to defend it, because I am convinced that the dangers with which it is threatened, in this country especially, arise more from failure to understand the necessary conditions of its survival than from any form of direct attack.

In concentrating my attention upon British political life and institutions, I have not been indifferent to the fate of parliamentary democracy in other countries. On the contrary, I believe that the future of democracy throughout the world depends in large measure upon the preservation and improvement of the British system of government. Moreover, our long and successful application of democratic methods suggests that an analysis of the British situation is most likely to bring out the essentials of parliamentary democracy.

The analysis attempted in the following pages may be justified on several grounds. To some minds, British political institutions are already in grave peril. I do not share that view, but it is none the less desirable to be on guard against complacency. Elements of danger have always existed, and in recent years new ones have emerged.

In the first place, it is difficult to resist the conclusion that there is a widespread lack of understanding, not only of our own political system, but also of the nature and conditions of political action as such. The very continuity and apparent stability of our political institutions have engendered a certain indifference to them, not unmingled with a measure of that contempt which familiarity often breeds. We are apt to take them for granted; we grumble at them, as is our habit; and we should probably rally to their defence if they were seriously attacked. Familiarity, however, is not the same thing as understanding; indifference, contempt, and unrestrained indulgence in the tendency we have to grumble, may all in their several ways weaken that which it is desired to preserve; and the instinctive rally against serious challenge is a poor substitute for the political intelligence which would obviate its necessity. It is this inadequate comprehension of the working of our political system which is responsible for excessive demands upon it, and for the resulting disillusionment. Too many people do not sufficiently understand either the nature of the British politician's work or the conditions under which he pursues his activities. They fail to penetrate beneath the superficialities of political life, and an atmosphere is created which is favourable to the growth of scepticism and cynicism.

In the second place, the extension of the functions of the State has given rise to real difficulties for all political systems, and to genuine doubts of the efficacy of existing political machinery and methods. Such doubts have been strengthened by the apparent inability of governments to cope with the manifold and complex problems of the post-war world. The political system, in this country as elsewhere, has been included in a general criticism of established institutions, fostered by economic distress. It has been held responsible for the failure to apply the so-called solutions which have found favour from time to time, numerous and incompatible though they have been. Since the coming of the world depression, especially, a demand has arisen for action as such—for getting something done, no matter what—and our political methods have been criticized as the main obstacle to its satisfaction. Other factors have been operative. Russian Communism may have few admirers here, but many who disapprove of its motives have a certain sympathy with some of its methods. The same is true of Italian Fascism; and many of those repelled by the one have been attracted by the other. However objectionable the incidentals may be, the spectacle of one group or party imposing its will ruthlessly upon the rest evokes a sympathetic response in the most diverse quarters. Both movements have given an impression of vigour, efficiency, and determination, qualities seemingly lacking under parliamentary régimes. They have a dramatic appeal which the latter do not possess and can never hope to acquire. The rise of other dictatorships has seemed to justify their derision of democratic principles and to confirm the view that there is a general movement away from parliamentary methods of government. These events abroad have exercised a two-fold influence. A tendency to worship at strange shrines has emerged; while the mood of pessimism about parliamentary institutions has deepened and feelings of alarm have been aroused. The growing volume of criticism; the clamour for some way out of economic distress and party confusion; the loss of confidence; all constitute additional elements of danger.

The absence of any direct challenge of importance should not blind us to the fact that there are other dangerous factors. "He goes furthest who knows not where he is going," Cromwell is alleged to have said. A quite genuine avowal of support for our political institutions may be combined with renunciation of the methods upon which they rest. A sincere belief in democracy may be accompanied by actions which strike at its very foundations. The last few years have witnessed a marked tendency to advocate policies and programmes which have no regard to the possible consequences upon our political system. Determination to achieve particular ends has led to a growing indifference to means. When prominent spokesmen of an important political party declare their intention to carry out a revolutionary policy by constitutional methods, it is certainly time to consider seriously whether or not that is possible, and what the effects of any attempt to carry out that intention are likely to be. In such circumstances, no further apology for this book need be advanced.

Doubtless there are many defects both in the form and the functioning of the British system of government. That is only to be expected, for men made it and men work it. But, however numerous and important the defects may be, it is of the first importance to preserve a sense of proportion. Dr.

G. P. Gooch recently made a timely plea for a "reasonable relativity" in these matters, and Professor Herbert Kraus has reminded us that, "No State form and no State constitution is absolutely ideal for a community of people. The criterion must always be whether under the existing circumstances it is comparatively the most agreeable and comparatively the best constitution, under which the people can live." Moreover, "the comparatively best constitution in the circumstances" is operated by fallible human beings.

Among the existing circumstances must be included the effects of historical development, not only upon the political forms but also upon the political temperament and habits of the people. The political systems of the countries of the world can be properly understood and soundly judged only in the light of their historical experiences. The events of the last few years are fully explicable only by reference to those experiences. A word of warning against generalisations based upon recent happenings abroad may not be out of place here. The establishment of the Union of Socialist Soviet Republics upon the ruins of the old Russian Empire; the supersession of parliamentary government in Italy and Germany and Austria; the dictatorships, naked or veiled, in Turkey or Poland, Hungary or Yugo-Slavia; do not in themselves provide any justification either for doubts about the value of British parliamentary democracy or for alarm about its future. As Mr. Walter Citrine has said, in one of his many able speeches on the subject, "Almost in every case where dictatorships have arisen the institutions of the country had either not been democratic institutions in the full sense as understood in this country, or the institutions had been so recent in origin, and had had so little time to become grafted into the consciousness of the people, that they had not become part of the national life."[1]

In the circumstances indicated, a re-examination of the British system of government is eminently desirable. This book has been written as a contribution to that end. I hope it may do something to remove popular misapprehensions; to indicate what can and what can not be done through the existing political machinery and by the customary methods; and, by clarifying the position, to counteract tendencies which may endanger, and strengthen those which may improve, the functioning of British political institutions. If it should succeed only in drawing attention to the need for a fuller and more authoritative exposition, it will have achieved its purpose.

The book is divided into two parts: in the first, I have endeavoured to state or to re-state the essentials of the British system of parliamentary government, and to indicate the conditions of its continuance; in the second, the argument is illustrated by a critical analysis of certain recent tendencies in British politics.

I have felt it necessary to refer briefly, in Chapter I, to the main characteristics of British constitutional and political development, and to re-interpret the central features of the existing political system. To this Chapter I have appended a note on the charge of dictatorship levelled against the Cabinet by Professor Ramsay Muir. In Chapters II and III, I have dealt at considerable length with the relatively neglected and all-important part played in the working of the

[1] Trades Union Congress, Brighton, September, 1933.

system by the political parties. Since the subject of British parliamentary government is so intimately bound up with the general subject of democracy, I have devoted Chapter IV to an interpretation of the meaning of democracy, and to a discussion of the extent to which our political institutions and practices conform to the democratic method. I have proceeded from an affirmation of the essentially democratic basis of our political system to a critical examination, in Chapters V and VI, of certain popular arguments purporting to show that the system is doomed to collapse, and to an elucidation of the conditions upon which it depends for its maintenance and improvement. Finally, in Part II, I have discussed some recent developments in British politics which are potentially dangerous to parliamentary government; the views and proposals associated with the names of Sir Stafford Cripps, Professor H. J. Laski and Mr. G. D. H. Cole; the attitude of the Labour, Conservative and Liberal parties; the emergence of Sir Oswald Mosley's Fascist movement; and the problems raised by the existence and possible growth of anti-parliamentary political parties.

I desire to express my thanks to the group of friends with whom I have been associated in political studies or public activities, and with whom, despite inevitable differences of opinion and changes of party allegiance, I have shared the hopes and anxieties of recent times. Without their encouragement this book would not have been written; without their insistence and help it would not have been published; and whatever value it may have is due in large measure to their advice and criticism.

My indebtedness to many distinguished writers on British political history and institutions is obvious. I can only express the hope that I have not omitted to give due acknowledgement in any particular instance.

R. BASSETT.

Frant, Sussex,
January, 1935.

CONTENTS

PART ONE

CHAPTER I

THE BRITISH POLITICAL SYSTEM

CHAPTER II

THE POLITICAL PARTIES (I)

CHAPTER III

THE POLITICAL PARTIES (II)

CHAPTER IV

DEMOCRACY

Chapter V

THE CONDITIONS OF CONTINUANCE (I)

Chapter VI

Demer

THE CONDITIONS OF CONTINUANCE (II)

PART TWO

RECENT TENDENCIES IN BRITISH POLITICS

PART ONE

CHAPTER I

THE BRITISH POLITICAL SYSTEM

1. *The Continuity of British Political Development*

CERTAIN primary facts of British political history can hardly be too often repeated. Our political system is the product of nearly nine hundred years of steady and relatively unbroken development. In that respect it is unique.[1] Periods of confusion and acute political tension have occurred; in earlier times, the evolution has been retarded and even rudely interrupted; but, invariably, the interruptions over, the slow process of constitutional development has been resumed at the point where it was broken off. Only once has the whole basis of the constitution been seriously challenged, and even then Cromwell's political insight led him to retain as much of the old as the conditions allowed, and to pave the way for its restoration. Profound as were its consequences in stimulating political thought, and in its influence upon the development of parties, the Puritan Revolution, from the constitutional standpoint, merely consolidated the

---

[1] "Some parts of it may be traced back to the woods of Germany; others, though much newer, are still several hundred years old; the whole outward framework of it is ancient; the inner part, though gradually modified, has never been changed upon system. Few such things have ever lasted so long; few such have ever undergone so much needful change with so little solution of continuity."— Bagehot, "The Chances for a long Conservative Régime in England," Vol. VII, *The Works and Life of Walter Bagehot*, p. 75.

gains secured prior to its outbreak.[1] The "Glorious Revolution" of 1688—our last—was essentially the defeat of an attempt to reverse or to divert the course of constitutional development. It was carried out as "constitutionally" as a revolution can be; and it introduced nothing new, save the Protestant Succession, even though it may be inaccurate to contend that "it made nothing law which had not been law before."

If the subsequent period alone is taken, few States have been fortunate enough to share our immunity from political upheaval. The British Constitution is the outstanding example of "gradualism." The process has been such that it is usually difficult and often impossible to say when a particular institution was first established, or a particular political practice first recognised.

"In every case the change, the step forward, has been by way of partial amendment of a 'going concern'."[2] The system has not been "planned;" it has not even been consciously anticipated, and hence it has never been authoritatively written down. From mediæval times, it has been continuously adapted, with greater or less success, to the practical needs of the moment. As has been so often said, it is not a creation, but a growth.

Its most striking characteristics spring from this primary fact of the long, slow, and continuous process

[1] "Apart from the immense effect which the Rebellion had in bringing the nation to political maturity, its net result, when all was over, was confined to a limited number of definite reforms, lying in the natural line of development, and carrying a long step forward the age-long process by which the supremacy of Parliament was established over legislation and taxation."—Sir Maurice Amos, *The English Constitution*, p. 51.

[2] Amos, *op. cit.* p. 52.

of constitutional and political growth. The absence of a written constitution, or of any special procedure for constitutional amendment, and the extensive basis in custom, make our political system remarkably adaptable. This elasticity has always been recognised as an important asset. The development proceeds, often imperceptibly, and the growth of new customs can modify the system in the future as it has done in the past. New situations can be met with relative facility; the recrudescence of old situations can be met, if necessary, by reversion to previous constitutional practices.

Drastic changes, however, have been few. Prognostications of ruin consequent upon impending change have been frequent enough, but, in the light of history, the changes that have seemed most drastic at the time have come to be regarded as modest and cautious. "Leaps in the dark" have appeared far less adventurous in retrospect. There has been, for instance, no plunge into "democracy," even if by that term is understood merely the participation of the mass of the people in the choice of representatives. In this connection, as in others, the process has been accomplished by stages, after considerable intervals of preparation, more or less adequate, and sometimes thought unduly prolonged.

That the adaptations considered necessary or desirable—amounting in sum to a transformation of the political system—have been effected, for the most part, by due process of law and without resort to violence is a significant fact, however much may be attributed to good fortune. It has not been due to an absence of issues arousing political passion, for the

c

political struggle has been intense throughout. Attention should also be directed to the far-reaching economic and social changes which have taken place during the course of this orderly evolution, and which have been reflected in political action. Developments of more serious import may arise, but the natural tendency to exaggerate the significance of immediate issues receives a wholesome correction if the changes and controversies of the past are recalled.

2. *Its Practical and Experimental Nature*

Political speculation has influenced development, but, throughout, the dominant considerations have been practical. Alike in constitutional and in general political matters, attention has been concentrated upon securing workable arrangements in regard to the more urgent and immediate problems. The wider issues or implications have not been pressed. This does not mean that they have been unappreciated, but that the scope of political controversy has been effectually limited, as a rule, to projects capable of being defended or opposed on practical grounds. As political experience has increased, there has developed a reluctance to push things to extremities. In this way, conflicts over general principles, invariably the most violent of conflicts, have played relatively little part in British political life. The bitterness of political controversy has thus been diminished, and the path to political advance cleared and smoothed.

Constitutionally, there has been no attempt to construct a complete system of government on the basis of any theoretical scheme. Old instruments have been adapted to new uses, and new instruments grafted on to the old, as occasion has seemed to require. Practical expedients have been devised to cope with changing circumstances, often without any formal changes in machinery. Old forms, indeed, have not been abolished unless they have appeared definitely obstructive, and their retention has not been without value. The "ancient show" has been kept, the "new reality" interpolated, whether secretly, as Bagehot said, or otherwise, is of secondary import. Old customs have fallen into desuetude; new ones have been developed. The central feature of our present system —what we call Cabinet Government—is almost wholly conventional.

Symmetrical perfection has not been sought, and numerous and curious anomalies remain. Perhaps the most striking and irritating of these is the House of Lords, which has been called "a case of arrested development."[1] Parliament came into being, not because of any democratic theories, or, indeed, of any pressure from below, but as a possible method of dealing more effectively with immediate government business. It gradually acquired further power by insisting upon effective remedies for practical grievances, and by taking advantage of particular situations. "The English people," it has been said, "did not invent their democratic institutions; English life developed, somehow or other, into democracy."[2] In no respect, perhaps, is the practical element more clearly shown than in matters relative to the liberty of the subject: effective legal remedies have been

[1] A. F. Pollard, *The Evolution of Parliament*, p. 300.
[2] Rudolf Kircher, *How They Do It in England*, p. 8.

consistently preferred to high-sounding declarations of rights.

The methods adopted may legitimately be described as experimental. Provisional measures designed to deal with emergency situations or novel problems, when tested and proved effective, have received a wider application; when proved unsuccessful, or no longer required, they have been discarded. The same is true of governmental machinery. Provisional decisions have tended to become permanent, and partial solutions the basis of further progress. Limitation of effort to the immediate and urgent has facilitated wider or final settlement. Often, the postponement of obstinate problems has enabled the appropriate remedy to be found and peaceably applied. There have been failures, of course, and numerous exceptions to the general method, but these have invariably provided further evidence of its wisdom.

3. *The Logic of British Methods*

The British political system is often criticised for its alleged lack of a logical basis, for its assumed confusion of conflicting principles. Some commentators, like Montesquieu, have, indeed, credited it with a symmetry and a maturity which it has never at any stage possessed; but more frequently it is regarded as formless and illogical, the product of accident rather than design. We are told that it is typical of the Englishman's habit of "muddling along somehow," doing what has to be done as it turns up, without vision and without plan; and that the resultant system is the most remarkable joint product of his "blundering through" and his good fortune. It is curious that a people who have had unrivalled political experience and have come to be regarded as the most politically-minded people in the world should be so willing to look upon themselves as a nation of "muddlers." It is an even more curious trait that a people whose political institutions have been admittedly so successful, and widely if sometimes rashly imitated, should regard their more eminent statesmen, either as muddle-headed, or where that hypothesis is too obviously fantastic, as tricksters. The paradox prompts reflection. The complacent acceptance of the uncomplimentary epithets suggests that they are not taken too seriously. None the less, however beneficial self-criticism may be, the practice of self-disparagement may be harmful.

It is appropriate to enquire whether in fact the criticisms are justified. The British system is not the product of any doctrinaire idealism; it has not been evolved according to specification, on untested principles; but it is not devoid of guiding principles, which have been educed from British experience, and consciously adhered to and applied. A system moulded and adapted in all its parts by the consistent practice of these methods must of necessity be something more than a mere hotch-potch of heterogeneous elements. What distinguishes the British system is that it is based upon tested principles of practical political action, and not upon the principles of unpractical idealism or pedantic formalism. Is there no logic in the methods which have produced it? Those methods are pre-eminently experimental. In politics, more perhaps than in any other branch of human endeavour, action has to be taken upon insufficient data, and upon working hypotheses which may have to be discarded. "Blunders" are all too frequent; but is there no logic in such "blundering through?" Is it not the same thing as asking whether there is no logic in the process of experimentation? It is true that the results of this method are complex. That is because politics is a matter of the utmost complexity: it is no sign of illogicality. The British system of government is not illogical merely because it lacks the simplicity of the abstract systems which are formulated by political "thinkers" without political experience, or merely because it lacks that symmetrical perfection aimed at by constitution-mongers past and present.

The experimental method, be it noted, does not dispense with "planning." The two things, so far from being inconsistent, are inseparable. There may be planning without a Plan on the grand scale. Indeed, the grandiose schemes of "national planners" are invariably examples of bad planning, whether that which is to be planned is a political system or an economic mechanism. The field covered is too large and complex; the hypotheses are more crude; the margin of error greater; and the consequences of failure more serious. Such proposals suggest a degree of confidence dangerous in politics, and are usually distinguished by the rigidity of form and spirit born of an unwarranted certainty. At their best, they only constitute "blundering" on the grand scale.

Nor does the experimental method imply lack of foresight: quite the reverse is true. Those who look ahead, but overlook what lies between the "is" and the "is-to-be," may be men of vision, but they are certainly unsafe guides. In fact, their vision is defective; they are, so to speak, too long-sighted. Those who oppose or refrain from taking a particular step solely because of the possible implications or ultimate consequences are politically obstructive. On the other hand, looking ahead does not necessitate jumping ahead; it does not justify neglect of the practical problems and difficulties; nor does it involve repudiation of the method of proceeding by way of limited practical projects, when anyone of these can be justified on its merits and tested by experience. It has been said that "nothing is so permanent as the provisional," and history is full of illustrations. France, for instance, has had ten Constitutions since 1789; the makers of the Constitution of 1875, in acute disagreement on general principles, were reluctantly compelled to confine themselves to the bare necessities of the immediate situation; and the product of their labours, provisional and incomplete, has lasted down to the present time. "Muddling along," after all, may be a misnomer for political common-sense; just as the "muddle-headedness" of distinguished statesmen may be nothing more than a wise refusal to give a false simplicity to matter which is complex, and may be indicative of a wider knowledge, a deeper sense of responsibility, and a greater clarity of thought, than their critics themselves possess.

4. *Effects upon Political Institutions and Habits*

One of the results of the practical and experimental development of British political institutions has been the avoidance of abrupt transitions, or the substitution of one general plan for another. There have been no clean sweeps involving good and bad alike. It has been possible to select from conflicting general schemes, and to combine elements of value taken from each. The combination has been feasible because it has been conducted on the practical plane. It has been possible to retain what has been found of practical service in previous arrangements, and to guard against weaknesses and dangers in new elements introduced. The experiments have been conducted under safeguards. It is noteworthy that the safeguards, i.e. the provisions for dealing with emergencies, which are proposed for the new Indian Constitution are analogous to those existent, if in abeyance, in our own. In essence, they constitute an application of precautions similar to those we have found necessary or desirable for ourselves. In this way, for example, the major dangers and defects of what is called "democracy" have been largely avoided. There are practical limits to the effective participation of the people in government, and there are limits to the participation of a legislative assembly in government. Both have been recognised. Precautions have been taken against divorcement of power and responsibility. On the whole, responsibility is placed where it can be effectively borne and enforced. Precipitate popular action is, as far as possible, prevented. The electorate functions as such intermittently, and its decisions can take effect only by processes which are not under its direct control. Its representatives have considerable scope for discretionary action. At the same time, the representative assembly has not been entrusted with powers it is obviously incapable of exercising effectively, and safeguards exist against abuse of its powers. Consequently, there is effective scope for leadership and expert guidance. From this standpoint, as from others, substance has been preferred to form, theoretical perfection subordinated to practical efficiency. Many illustrations of these facts might be given. Among them may be mentioned our electoral system, designed to secure a definite decision by the voters rather than a mathematically accurate reflection of all shades and differences of opinion; our retention of royal prerogatives, which may be called into play in times of emergency or threatened breakdown, whether they be exercisable by the monarch in person or by his Ministers; the power of dissolution which is so vital a link in our system; and even the continued existence of the House of Lords as a check, whether satisfactory or otherwise, upon the abuse of power by the popular assembly.

British political history has produced other notable results. It is obvious that a people generations of whom have been born and bred in conditions of relative political tranquillity will have acquired habits different from those of peoples less happily situated. "Blundering" methods have both been rendered possible by, and in turn promoted, political stability. Among such a people, the tradition of orderly political life is a force to be reckoned with. For centuries, a considerable and ever-growing proportion of the people has consciously exercised a measure of political power; and a smaller proportion has enjoyed opportunities of participating in the actual work of government. No nation has had so long an experience of representative political institutions; none has had greater opportunities of acquiring the secrets of their successful working. In such circumstances, the general level of political intelligence is bound to be higher than in countries to which representative institutions are still a novelty. Experience counts for a very great deal. Moreover, our representative institutions are the product of our political habits and experiences; they have sprung out of our national life; they are part and parcel of it, have grown and developed along with it.[1] Other forms of parliamentary government have been set up in most cases in relatively recent times, and often as a result of revolution. All have been influenced in varying degrees by our example. Attempts have been made to copy our institutions. The conditions out of which the latter sprang, the conditions in which they have developed, could not be reproduced. Our political habits and methods, upon which our institutions depend, have been insufficiently understood, and are, perhaps, not easily acquired. Time and practice are requisite. The point, an old one, is worth recalling in connection with political happenings abroad. It is not without its significance for ourselves, for the lessons have to be learned anew by each generation.

5. *The Existing System : its Unitary Nature*

A re-statement of certain major features of the existing political system is a necessary preliminary

---

[1] It is not surprising that British Fascists are desperately anxious to show that parliamentary institutions are not "particularly adapted to the English genius," and that "Fascism is a movement no more foreign to the British genius than was Dutch Parliamentarism, French Republicanism, or German Socialism." Their efforts in this connection are amusing, vide, e.g. James Drennan, " B.U.F.," pp. 287–290. It is unfortunate for these fervent patriots

to the central argument of this book. The legal frame-work of the system does not call for our detailed attention: it has been described a hundred times. Nor need we linger over the functions of the various organs of government. It is in respect of the relations between these organs, and in regard to the motive power or powers, that differences of view and of emphasis arise. Here, interpretation is requisite, and a re-statement of the position is necessary to the succeeding argument.

It is significant that the terms "Cabinet," "Parliamentary," "Party" and "Democratic," are applied indiscriminately to our system of government: they are treated as synonymous. The fact is, of course, that Cabinet, Parliament, Party and Electorate, are intimately and inseparably connected. The tendency to make an artificial separation between them is the root of much misunderstanding: they are distinguishable, but not separate.

The British system is admittedly complex, and reference has already been made to the variety of elements which it comprises. But one of the most important things about it is that in spite of its real complexity, and the apparently conflicting elements, it is essentially a unity. The various elements are fused into an effective working whole. There is no such separation of governmental powers as obtains, for instance, in the United States of America. On the contrary, there is a high degree of concentration of power and responsibility, and it is that which gives our

that their creed should oblige them to attack, in our system of parliamentary government, the greatest of our national achievements.

system a strength as yet unattained by other forms or instances of representative government.

The explanation is to be found partly in the historical evolution of the system. All branches of English Government have a common source in the Crown. Originally, all the powers of the national State were vested in the King personally, and that is still the formal position.[1] The actual power of the monarch, of course, has largely disappeared; it is limited now, in normal circumstances, although only in such circumstances, to the extent to which the monarch can influence his Ministers. But the fact of kingship remains. The power of "The Crown" remains; it has scarcely been restricted since the seventeenth century; and, on balance, it has been greatly extended. What has happened is that the exercise of kingship has been transferred, by the development of constitutional customs, from the monarch to Ministers responsible to Parliament, and, through Parliament, to the electorate. In Dicey's well-known phrase, "the prerogatives of the Crown have become the prerogatives of the people." Parliament, for excellent reasons, is usually looked upon as the centre of our political system. It consists, however, of King, Lords and Commons. It was called into existence by the Crown, and the King and the King's Council (of which the Cabinet is now the effective part) have never been separated from it.[2] The Crown, the executive government, has

[1] "The influence of a common origin pervades every branch of English government, and behind all its specific functions there lies a fundamental unity symbolised by the Crown." . . . "It is not a mere form that all powers, executive, legislative, and judicial, are vested in the Crown."—A. F. Pollard, *The Evolution of Parliament*, pp. 238–239.

[2] On this point, and related issues, see Pollard, *op. cit.* p. 244 *et seq.*

never been cut off from the legislature. If the Crown and Parliament are thought of as separate, it becomes difficult to get a true picture of the "finely balanced relationship" which exists between the executive and the legislature; and that relationship is of the utmost importance.

6. *The Relationship between the Cabinet and Parliament*

The great problem of representative or democratic institutions is how to combine popular control with strong, efficient, and stable government. It is because the British system does provide a working synthesis, however imperfect, of the two things that it has met in the past with so large a measure of success. One of the keys to the system is found in what Bagehot called "the close union and nearly complete fusion of the executive and legislative powers." That has been effected by entrusting the powers of the Crown to the Cabinet, i.e. a body of Ministers drawn from, and responsible to, Parliament.

It is not a matter of the executive being subordinate to the legislature, or vice versa, but of an intimate union between them. The Cabinet Ministers, as a rule, are members of one or other of the Houses of Parliament; they are, in a sense, representatives of Parliament; and they are responsible to the House of Commons for their exercise of executive power. The Cabinet must enjoy the confidence of the House of Commons; it must secure its continuous support; it cannot continue in office save on those terms. On the other hand, the Cabinet is not the mere agent of Parliament, or of the House of Commons; it does not constitute a "committee of Parliament"; its members are not appointed by Parliament. They are much more than representatives responsible *to* Parliament; they are also, and primarily, Ministers of the Crown, responsible *for* the government of the country. As such, they guide and up to a point determine Parliament's activities. The responsibility for the initiation and making of laws rests primarily, and now almost exclusively, upon them. Special responsibilities are borne in the sphere of finance. In modern times, Government business has to an increasing extent occupied Parliament's time, and the arrangement of parliamentary business is left largely in the Cabinet's hands. Legislative proposals have little or no chance of being carried into law unless sponsored by the Cabinet. Increasingly, the details of legislation are left to Ministers, and settled by administrative orders and regulations.

These powers, however, are exercised with Parliament's consent. They are powers conferred or acquiesced in by Parliament, and revocable by Parliament. This aspect of the matter is often overlooked. But the Cabinet, normally, has one weapon of great importance at its disposal. It can appeal from a particular House of Commons to those who elect the House of Commons, by advising a dissolution of Parliament. This power gives the Cabinet a certain measure of independence of any particular Parliament. It gives it a strength not possessed, for example, by the executive government in France, where the power of dissolution has been in abeyance; a strength more commensurate with its responsibilities. It limits the possibilities of divorcement of the legislature from the electorate; provides a check upon the abuse of power by a relatively irresponsible body; and gives scope for leadership. Like all other powers, it may be abused, but it is none the less valuable.[1] It brings the executive government into more direct relations with the people, and a General Election becomes, in large measure, the election of a Government.

This element of independence is strengthened by the method of the Cabinet's appointment. Nominally, and in law, the Ministers are the King's servants, appointed and dismissed by him. In actual practice, the King merely appoints the Prime Minister, and entrusts him with the task of selecting all the other members of the Ministry, those who are to be in the Cabinet, and those who are not. Normally, the monarch has no power of choice in the appointment of the Prime Minister: the party system, as a rule, deprives him of any alternative. The House of Commons can make it impossible for a Cabinet, or for an individual Minister, to remain in office. Nearly always the predominant party in the House can determine who is to be the Prime Minister, although there is another very powerful influence; that exerted by the members of the party outside Parliament, and, indeed, by the general public. It is quite conceivable that a politician, popular in his party, and in the country generally, may not be the person preferred by the majority of

[1] It is significant to note that a strong demand for revival of the power of dissolution has arisen in France, where the instability of ministries, and the general weakness of the executive government, have contributed greatly to the development of one of the most critical situations which the Third Republic has yet encountered. The effective restoration of the power of dissolution is probable in the near future.

his fellow party members in Parliament. Even so, his parliamentary colleagues may make him their leader, because otherwise they might lose support in the country, or risk the unity of their party. There is something to be said for the view that the man who chooses the Cabinet is himself often chosen by the people. A General Election is, to some extent, the election of a Prime Minister; and sometimes the popular choice is very clearly indicated, as in the case of Gladstone in 1880. In any event, the House of Commons cannot determine who the other Ministers shall be. It may exercise considerable influence, but, in fact, the other Ministers are the nominees neither of the House of Commons itself nor of the dominant party in the House.

7. *Misinterpretations of the Position of the Cabinet*

The Cabinet, however, is neither the master nor the servant of Parliament, and both alike are subject to the electorate. We are sometimes told that "the Cabinet absolutely controls Parliament." Professor Ramsay Muir has given the weight of his authority to the view, expressed in many quarters and in various forms, that there is a "Cabinet dictatorship." Others complain of the weakness of the executive government under our system: they object to the control exercised by Parliament over the Cabinet. These are extreme and incompatible views, but, so far as the post-war situation is concerned, the second line of criticism is more tenable than the first. "Cabinet dictatorship" is a myth: so is the associated "autocracy" of the Prime Minister. In the appendix to this chapter, further reference is made to Professor Muir's argument in these connections. Let it suffice here to suggest that both views are based, though in disproportionate degree, upon an unjustifiable antithesis between Cabinet and Parliament.[1] The Cabinet is an integral part of Parliament, and it is powerless without its parliamentary majority. It should not be artificially separated from its supporters in Parliament and in the country. Talk of "Cabinet dictatorship" implies a degree of homogeneity and isolation which no Cabinet enjoys. A Cabinet can strengthen its position in Parliament only by concession to opponents or by appeal to the electorate, and it is surely misleading to characterise such an appeal as an exercise of dictatorial power. A Cabinet with an uncertain majority is necessarily weak. Those who complain of executive weakness often overlook the party situation, and it is there, often enough, that the explanation is to be found. Frequently, it is a case of party rather than Cabinet weakness.

---

[1] It may be noted that the party or parties in opposition, whichever they may happen to be, tend to over-stress the power of the Cabinet, and they are loud in their protests against the ruthlessness of the majority. Supporters of the Cabinet, on the other hand, shew a tendency to exaggerate the obstructive, restrictive, powers of the House of Commons over against the Cabinet. "Back-benchers" of all parties are apt to complain of what they call "Cabinet dictatorship." Those of the Government party or parties are inclined to be more prominent in this respect than those of the Opposition party or parties; their hopes having been the greater, their disappointment is the more intense. An Opposition party, having prospects of securing a majority in the not too distant future, is inclined to temper its denunciations of Cabinet "dictatorship," having no objection to wielding the powers of the Cabinet itself. But a party with no prospects of that kind has a marked tendency to let itself go on the subject: it is tempted to demand strong parliamentary control over any Cabinet, and, with that end in view, to over-stress the authority of the Cabinet.

8. *The Connecting Link of Party*

Criticisms of the "dictatorial" power of the Cabinet are in reality criticisms of party, and sometimes merely of the particular party in power. The desire for an "independent House of Commons" is an expression of the natural dissatisfaction of the minority or minorities, and of the "back-bench" member. Under the British system, there is no ground for fear of "Cabinet dictatorship." There may be a danger of *Party* dictatorship, but that opens up other issues, which will be discussed later. A more real danger is that the Cabinet may be unduly weakened. Weakness and instability of the executive is the great flaw in most systems of representative government. It is the point of danger, as continental experience has so clearly shown. The great merit of the British system, as has been suggested, is that in practice it has provided a relatively strong and stable executive. That is attributable in large measure to its origins and to the nature of its development. The use of the prerogative of dissolution is also of much importance. The central explanation, however, is to be found in the nature of the British party structure, and the maintenance of an effective executive is dependent upon the future of parties. Parliament itself, be it remembered, cannot govern. Under a parliamentary system, therefore, efficient government depends upon the harmonious co-operation of the executive government and the Parliament to which it is responsible. It is party which makes such co-operation possible. Party is the connecting link between the executive and the legislature, between Cabinet and Parliament. It is the connecting link also between Cabinet and people, and between Parliament and people. It is party, moreover, which provides the chief motive power in any system of government; and the clue to the comparatively successful working of the British system of government is to be found in the British party system.

APPENDIX

" CABINET DICTATORSHIP "

WHAT are the facts about the alleged dictatorship of the Cabinet? Professor Ramsay Muir's references to the subject in his *How Britain is Governed*, and elsewhere, merit attention. "The truth," he contends, "is that— except when it is not in command of a clear majority— the Cabinet absolutely controls Parliament."[1] The "most distinctive feature of the British system is the concentration of all power and all responsibility, administrative, legislative, and even (in the last resort) judicial, in the hands of 'the Government,' so long as it commands a majority in the House of Commons. This dictatorship (for such it essentially is) may be wielded by the heads of any organised political party which is able to win a majority of seats in the House of Commons by the skilful use of electioneering devices, even if this majority of seats represents (as it often does) a minority of votes."[2]

The impression conveyed by these remarks, it is suggested, is highly misleading. It is quite true, as Professor Muir contends, that the Cabinet in practice virtually monopolises the time of the House of Commons; that Government Bills, or Bills approved by the Government, alone stand any chance of becoming law; and that, in normal circumstances, and in so far as

[1] p. 16, *op. cit.*   [2] p. 26, *op. cit.*

24

time permits, Government Bills do become law. It is true also that, by long established practice, no proposal for taxation or expenditure can be made except by a Minister of the Crown. These and other facts might seem to justify the view that there is a Cabinet "dictatorship," but these things are done by the Cabinet as a consequence of parliamentary decisions. The limitations placed upon the financial powers of members of the House of Commons, for instance, are the result of decisions by the House of Commons. They are self-imposed limitations, embodied in Standing Orders.[1] The Cabinet's control over the time of the House of Commons is exercisable only with the consent of the House. Consent has to be obtained if the Cabinet wishes to take up more of the time of the House than the Standing Orders already allow, and, as a matter of fact, the general business of the House, including the allotment of time, is arranged, so far as possible, after consultation and by agreement with the party or parties in opposition.

So far from the Cabinet exercising a "dictatorship," it is dependent all the time upon the support of its party majority in the House of Commons. Its power is continuously limited by the necessity of maintaining that majority, and its general policy may have to be modified accordingly. Its Bills may have to be modified. Professor Muir grants this, but says that "if the Cabinet has a stable majority, the modification will only happen by its own consent." It is true that Cabinet consent to the modification is requisite, but the Cabinet often has to consent, or sacrifice the

---

[1] The most important of them date back to the early years of the eighteenth century.

measure, unless it is prepared to risk defeat and its possible consequences.

Professor Muir makes the "dictatorship" of the Cabinet conditional upon the support of a majority. It is a rather far-reaching qualification, for without a majority the Cabinet, of course, is powerless; but its effect is minimised, and the allegation of "dictatorship" rendered plausible, by the "automatic" or "docile" nature attributed to the majority. It is said that "so long as the Government commands a docile majority in Parliament, its power is practically unlimited and uncontrolled." But when does a Cabinet "command" a majority? Is a majority ever "docile," or "automatic?" Surely only under conditions such as obtain under the régimes of Mussolini or Hitler. Professor Muir has had, it is believed, some experience of the difficulties of getting a parliamentary minority to act in unison, and it would be unwise to assume that the task is easier in the case of a majority. That members of Parliament are deficient in a spirit of independence is very frequently asserted, especially by the Opposition of ministerialists. Paradoxically, the Opposition members denounce the Cabinet just as frequently for giving way to the clamour of their unruly and extremist followers. There is no basis for the assumption of "docility." Ministers and "Whips" would doubtless tell a very different story. It is true that, as a rule, members hesitate "to carry their independence to the point of open revolt," but it is only political common-sense to exhaust every means of persuasion and influence before openly producing a breach in the party ranks. If it is the private member who is more often the person persuaded, that is only to be expected from the nature of the case.

Moreover, it would be stupid to run the risk of weakening or even overthrowing a "government" to whom one gives general support, unless the matter in dispute is considered of such vital importance that everything else must be subordinated to it. A superficial appearance of tranquillity and docility is, no doubt, produced, but surely no student or practitioner of politics is deceived by it. Furthermore, Professor Muir allows that, even with a docile majority behind it, the Cabinet is restrained "by the fear of alienating public opinion and therefore losing its power at the next General Election." That constitutes a highly powerful limitation upon its so-called "dictatorship." Nor is it merely, as is suggested, a case of "not alienating that fluctuating margin of voters who have it in their power to turn the scale in a few constituencies." It is a question of dealing with a complex of groups of various kinds, any or all of which may have to be considered at any particular time on any particular issue. The Cabinet's power, with or without a *Party* majority, is continuously limited by the necessity of securing the support of a majority in the House of Commons, and, normally, also in the House of Lords, and by the necessity of securing the assent, or not alienating the support, of a majority of the electorate. In the House of Commons itself, power resides essentially with the majority, not with the Cabinet. Indeed, the Cabinet and its supporters cannot be artificially separated in the manner implicit in the phrase "Cabinet dictatorship." The members of the Cabinet, after all, are leaders or influential members of their party or parties.

It seems clear from the general argument of Professor Muir's book that his real objection is not so much to what he calls the "dictatorship" of the Cabinet, as to a position in which the Cabinet has the support of a majority composed of members of one party only. The central point of his attack, therefore, is the two-party system. He is clearly anxious to maintain efficient Cabinet Government, but while he recognises fully the need for harmony between the executive and Parliament, and also the necessity and value of party, he nevertheless objects to that harmony being attained by means of a one-party Cabinet backed by a one-party majority in the House of Commons. In such circumstances, his interesting argument has to follow a rather narrow path, and it is difficult to resist the impression that it has been influenced by the situation in recent years of the party with which Professor Muir is so closely associated. Whatever its merits may be (and further reference will be made to it), the case is weakened rather than strengthened by the unjustifiable attribution of dictatorial powers to the Cabinet.[1]

[1] The conclusions drawn by Sir Courtenay Ilbert on this subject are valuable. He says that "in the common talk about party tyranny, and about the despotism exercised by cabinets or whips, there is, to speak plainly, much nonsense and much cant. A member of Parliament is not a puppet, but a human being, very human, influenced by the same kind of considerations and actuated by the same kind of motives as his fellow mortals outside the walls of the House . . . no one knows better than a political leader what arts of persuasion, what tactics of conciliation and compromise, are required to keep a party together. He knows that too severe a strain must not be put on party allegiance, that diversity of opinions within the party ranks must be recognised, and that on many points the lines of division between different opinions by no means coincide with the lines of division between different political parties. And leaders and followers alike are aware that they cannot afford to disregard public opinion outside Parliament, that they must watch

Equally misleading is the connected view of the position of the Prime Minister. It is difficult, no doubt, to generalise on the subject, for so much depends upon the individual concerned and the circumstances. The actual power wielded by the Premier varies with each holder of the office, and with the same holder at different times. Gladstone's authority was far greater in the Cabinet of 1886 than in that of 1880–1885, and much less in the Cabinet of 1892–1894. The Prime Minister may be only "primus inter pares"; he may be much more than that; but he is seldom or never the "autocrat" or "potentate" he is often assumed to be. As a rule, he enjoys exceptional authority among his Cabinet colleagues. That authority, however, is only in part derived from his position as head of the ministry. As the individual entrusted by the King with the task of forming an administration, he is, clearly, in a special position; but when it is stated that he "not only selects the Ministers and assigns to them their offices, he can dismiss any of them, or transfer them from one office to another," we have a description of the constitutional forms and not of the political realities. Normally, the Premier is in these matters anything but a free agent. His power of choice is restricted in many ways, most of them obvious enough. The present Prime Minister pointed out in 1909 that "however arbitrary the present method may seem, Premiers have not an absolute freedom of choice regarding their subordinate Ministers."[1] After personal experience of the position, he would probably emphasise rather than

---

its variations and fluctuations, and guide their actions accordingly." (*Parliament*, p. 165, *et seq.*)

[1] J. R. MacDonald, *Socialism and Government*, Vol. II, p. 31.

modify his statement. The most autocratically-minded Prime Minister has to modify his personal wishes, as memoirs and biographies abundantly testify. Anything less like an "autocrat" than a British Prime Minister it would be difficult to conceive. Professor Muir says that "so long as he controls a majority in the House of Commons, he wields all the powers of Parliament as well as all the powers of the Crown." This qualification, as we have seen, is all-important. There is another. " But it is necessary that the Prime Minister should carry his colleagues in the Cabinet, or a large majority of them, along with him; because, while they are his nominees, they are also the leading members of his party, and all his power will disappear if he cannot count upon the support of his party." Take the first point. He must carry his Cabinet colleagues along with him, and it can hardly be assumed that they will be distinguished for "docility." Indeed, the existence of "Cabinet dissensions" is constantly affirmed. It is true that the wish is often father to the allegation. " As a general rule," said Bagehot, "nothing can be less worth attention than rumours as to the divisions in Cabinets. Every one knows how they are generated in the smoking-rooms of clubs and of the House of Commons." But, as Bagehot pointed out, all Cabinets are divided. "Fifteen clever men never agree about anything : but how they are divided it is rarely possible to know, and then only under a pledge of secrecy." The measures proposed by the Cabinet are usually the result of compromise ; and the Prime Minister, like any other member of the Cabinet, is often obliged to concede his individual judgment. Sir Robert Peel, who had as high a conception of his position and duties as any man who has ever held the office, not only admitted the fact but energetically defended its implications.[1] In some cases, the Prime Minister's primary qualification for his office has been a gift for getting difficult people to work together;[2] and at all times, it is a necessary qualification.

Secondly, the Prime Minister's power is dependent upon the support of his party. That is very largely the case. The Prime Minister has, continuously, to maintain his position as leader of his party, or sometimes, of a combination of parties. In order to do so, he frequently has to modify, and sometimes to sacrifice, his own views. A person in such a position cannot properly be described as an "autocrat" or "potentate," whatever the precise signification of the latter term may be. The notion of the Prime Minister as a person

[1] "Is there any one in this House so ignorant as to suppose that on all questions Cabinet ministers, who yield to the decision of their colleagues, speak and act in Parliament in strict conformity with the opinions they have expressed in the Cabinet? If ministers are to be taunted on every occasion that they hold opinions in the Cabinet different from what they do in this House, and if Parliament is to be made the scene of these taunts, I believe I should not be going too far in saying the House would have time for little else. It is the uniform practice with all governments." (Quoted in Bagehot's *Character of Sir Robert Peel*.)

[2] Mr. Keith Feiling has written of Disraeli's "Arch-Mediocrity," the Earl of Liverpool, "Inheriting a legacy of vendettas, for fifteen years he harnessed them to one service—the irritable genius of Canning, the despotic Wellesley, the insensate rectitude of the Home Secretary Sidmouth, and the righteous ambition of Peel." (*Sketches in Nineteenth Century Biography*.)

"It was said in after days that Asquith had no party in his own Government. He held the balance so evenly between Left wing and Right wing, and was so fair to all that none could claim him as a partisan. This was true, but it required a certain suppression of the old Adam in a man who was given to strong preferences and antipathies. There were times when the air seemed to vibrate with his unspoken comments."—J. A. Spender, *Life of Lord Oxford and Asquith*, p. 200.

habitually dictating the policy of his Government is hopelessly wide of the mark, and it is of some importance that its widespread vogue should be checked. However, it would be going too far, in our opinion, to say that "the whole strength of the Prime Minister rests upon the fact that he is a party Chief." It is not quite true that "if the party revolts against his leadership in an instant all his power melts away."

A Prime Minister does not derive his authority wholly from his party. His relations with his party are, as a rule, intimate. As a rule, he has been closely identified with his party over a period of years, and his party always derives some part of its power from him. The outcome of a revolt against his leadership may well be a breach in the party. He is not the servant any more than he is the master of his party, and his influence usually extends beyond its ranks. The real source of whatever authority a Prime Minister may possess is to be found in his own political ability. It is virtually impossible for a British Prime Minister to be a mediocrity. Disraeli's "transient and embarrassed phantom" was, perhaps, the one mediocrity in a long list of Premiers, and for his appearance in it the responsibility rests exclusively upon George IV.

CHAPTER II

1. *The Importance and Necessity of Parties*

THE working of any system of representative government is in large measure determined by the nature of
the political parties which operate it, and by changes
in the party structure. Neglect of this fact goes far
to account for the relative ill-success of representative
institutions abroad. Any political system should be
framed and judged in relation to the forces which work
it. A constitution which ignores this conditioning
factor cannot function as intended.

The British system of government—the product of
British experience—is largely the product of British
party life. The existence of parties has been a condition
of its development; and the nature of the parties has
influenced the nature of that development. The part
played by party, indeed, has been vital. It is not
only a matter of the struggles between parties: it
is also the fact of their existence. Without party, the
struggle against absolute monarchy could not have
been won. Without party, Cabinet government could
not have developed.[1] Not until political parties were

[1] " . . . the secret of the English Constitution as it was developed
in the course of the eighteenth century was the steady confidence
reposed by the parliamentary majority in the Cabinet of the day.
If that confidence is withdrawn every few months government becomes unstable, and men cry out for a despotism, old or new. In

organised could the personal power of the monarch be restricted and gradually reduced to its present limits. Even now, as we shall point out, changes in the party system may increase the personal power of the monarch. The emergence, development, and consolidation of the Cabinet system of government proceeded *pari passu* with the rise and development of political parties. In the critical periods of our constitutional evolution, the monarchs of England all recognised the importance of party. William III and Anne, no less anxious than George III to maintain their personal authority, detested party as heartily as he did. George III judged soundly that the weakening of party was an indispensable preliminary to the application of his conceptions of government; but, from the standpoint of his political aims, he was too constitutional a King. Unprepared to set up frankly as an autocrat, he endeavoured to work within the machinery of parliamentary institutions. Consequently, under the conditions of representative government, he was himself compelled to form a party, and, in the outcome, revived and consolidated party government.

George III's failure helps to bring out the important fact that political parties are a necessary corollary of representative government. "There never was an election without a party," wrote Bagehot:

"The House of Commons lives in a state of perpetual potential choice: at any moment it can choose a ruler and

---

eighteenth-century England the requisite confidence of Parliament in the Cabinet could have been obtained in no other manner than through the bond of a party loyalty held in common by the Cabinet and by the majority of the House of Commons."—Professor G. M. Trevelyan, Romanes Lecture.

dismiss a ruler. And therefore party is inherent in it, is bone of its bone, and breath of its breath."[1]

The widespread criticism and condemnation of parties makes it desirable to insist upon their indispensability. In any circumstances, co-operation with those of similar interests or similar opinions is natural; and it is also necessary if the individual is to exercise the maximum degree of political influence. That is the case under any system of government, and it is much more the case where political power is widely diffused. Under representative institutions, the isolated individual, however favourably situated in other respects, is virtually helpless. For all save a few outstanding personalities, political isolation or aloofness means political impotence; and in most cases the great "independents" themselves would be more effective if they abandoned their "independence."[2]

[1] *The English Constitution*, p. 125 (1928 Edition).

[2] "Where men are not acquainted with each other's principles, nor experienced in each other's talents, nor at all practised in their mutual habitudes and dispositions by joint efforts in business; no personal confidence, no friendship, no common interest, subsisting among them; it is evidently impossible that they can act a public part with uniformity, perseverance, or efficacy. In a connexion, the most inconsiderable man, by adding to the weight of the whole, has his value, and his use; out of it, the greatest talents are wholly unserviceable to the public. No man, who is not inflamed by vainglory into enthusiasm, can flatter himself that his single, unsupported, desultory, unsystematic endeavours are of power to defeat the subtle designs and united cabals of ambitious citizens. When bad men combine, the good must associate; else they will fall, one by one, an unpitied sacrifice in a contemptible struggle.

It is not enough in a situation of trust in the commonwealth, that a man means well to his country; it is not enough that in his single person he never did an evil act, but always voted according to his conscience, and even harangued against every design which he apprehended to be prejudicial to the interests of his country. This innoxious and ineffectual character that seems formed upon a plan of apology and disculpation falls miserably short of the mark of public duty. That duty demands and requires that what is right

"Organised co-operation among those who broadly think alike," says Professor Ramsay Muir, "is the essential condition of achievement; and organised co-operation is party."[1] As the electorate has grown, so party organisation has developed. The connection is clearly seen in our British political history: the successive extensions of the franchise have been followed by new departures in party organisation and activity. For "democracy without party is like a crowd without a purpose."[2] It has been written that "A nation,

> Where none was for a party,
> But all were for the State,

would be no more, upon the most favourable computation, than an impotent babel of virtuous voices."[3] Such a situation, however, cannot be attained; party cannot be so easily eliminated; in some form or other it will always exist. A so-called "non-party" State would be, in fact, a State comprising a multitude of parties or groups. Those who clamour for the abolition of parties are crying for the moon; and there is a great deal in the contention that they "seldom mean more than that everybody ought to think as they do, or be forbidden to express an opinion."[4]

---

should not only be made known, but made prevalent; that what is evil should not only be detected, but defeated. When the public man omits to put himself in a situation of doing his duty with effect, it is an omission that frustrates the purposes of his trust almost as much as if he had formally betrayed it. It is surely no very rational account of a man's life, that he has always acted right; but has taken special care to act in such a manner that his endeavours could not possibly be productive of any consequence."— Burke, *Thoughts on the Cause of the Present Discontents.*

[1] *How Britain is Governed*, p. 117.
[2] J. R. MacDonald, *Socialism and Government*, Vol. II, p. 13.
[3] F. Scott Oliver, *The Endless Adventure*, Vol I, p. 96.
[4] Ramsay Muir, *Is Democracy a Failure ?*

Under free representative institutions, there can be no such thing as "non-party" government; the use of the term is very misleading; it is, in fact, an euphemism for coalition government.[1]

2. Criticisms of Party

Parties, of course, are not an unmixed blessing; and their own behaviour is, no doubt, largely responsible for their unpopularity. It may well be said that parties have been the worst enemies of party. There will be occasion later on to refer to these aspects of the subject, but, here again, a "reasonable relativity" is desirable. The incidental defects of party should not be allowed to obscure either its necessity or its merits: party must be distinguished from the abuses of partisanship. Moreover, the unpopularity of party, whatever its justification, may provide a cover for attack upon those institutions of which party is an inevitable accompaniment, i.e. upon parliamentary government itself.

Hostility to party was natural in absolute monarchs, and in British monarchs desirous of maintaining or extending their personal authority. It is natural also to all those who aim at personal or party dictatorship. Parties cannot be eliminated, but criticism of party

[1] In this connection, it is much to be regretted that some devotedly democratic supporters of the present "National" Government should loosely employ expressions and arguments which are part of the stock-in-trade of Fascist movements. It is important to distinguish between the co-operation in government of different political parties or groups, and the repudiation of party as such which is implied in advocacy of non-party government. The first is legitimate from the standpoint of parliamentary democracy; the second is not, and only plays into the hands of the opponents of parliamentary institutions.

E

as such can be exploited in the interests of a party which identifies itself with the State, and claims to represent "national" as opposed to "sectional" interests, but which in fact is anxious to impose its will dictatorially upon the rest of the community.

Denunciation of political parties may serve as a mask for the forcible triumph of a new party and suppression of the others. Modern dictatorships, in their Italian, Russian, and German forms, are dictatorships of one party. Hitler's "totalitarian" State is not a "non-party" State; it is the result of the forcible suppression or absorption by one party of the rest. Even so, a one-party State comes to much the same thing as a "non-Party" State. It is worth remembering that a one-party State is a State in which political changes are the result of the conflicts of personalities or groups, conducted, for the most part, "behind the scenes." This is just as true of the Communist Party dictatorship in Russia, of the Fascist Party dictatorship in Italy, and of Hitler's Germany to-day, as it was true of Tsarist Russia or of the France of Louis XIV. It is incompatible with parliamentary government.

Criticism of political parties springs largely from the notion that they "divide the nation." "They live by noise and fury, signifying nothing." The political system seems to be based, in Lord Balfour's words, on "systematised differences and unresolved discords." The struggle of parties looms large, and, on a superficial view, they appear to be disturbers of tranquillity and agents of disunion. So, undoubtedly, they sometimes are; for it is true that in the contest for power, points of disagreement are emphasised, and points of agreement largely ignored. It is also true that there is much insincerity; parties have an apparently ineradicable tendency to credit their opponents with evil motives, incompetence and stupidity. Admittedly, partisanship is carried much too far. Opposition has even been held to be a duty for "the Opposition," with most unfortunate results, not least for those who have acted on the maxim. But, although these things are true and important, they are only the secondary aspects of the matter, and are to a large extent remediable.

Party is essentially a unifying force. The narrower its basis the less the power of unification, but, however narrow a party's basis may be, it represents a measure of co-operation. No one can enter or belong to a political party without to some degree subordinating his own particular views or interests. Every political party involves the pooling of individual ideas, the adjustment of personal and sectional interests, and a measure of compromise in order to secure the maximum degree of common agreement. It may obstruct further progress in that direction: that is a danger to which parties are always liable. But the notion that parties are uncalled-for intruders in a state of political harmony is, of course, fantastic. They do not divide "the people." Without them—if one can conceive the impossible—there would hardly be any such thing as a "people" in a political sense. Without them, there would be a chaos of isolated individuals with conflicting interests and views.[1] A two-party

[1] "If parties cause some evils, they avert or mitigate others. To begin with, parties are inevitable. No free large country has been without them. No one has shewn how representative government could be worked without them. They bring order out of the chaos

system, for instance, does not divide the nation or parliament into "two disciplined armies"; on the contrary, it carries the process of unification almost as far as it can be carried. The obvious facts are that unanimity is an unattainable ideal, and that it is difficult enough to get even a majority of people to agree on a general course of action or on a particular proposal.

3. The " Two-Party System " and Cabinet Government

One result of the gradual but continuous development of the British system of government has been the continuity of the great political parties. The relatively simple party structure operative in less democratic days has been adapted to the wider electorate. The new elements have been assimilated by the old party structure. In countries where there has been a relatively sharp transition to representative institutions, the political parties have naturally presented a much more confusing picture. But, in this country, one of the most striking features of our political life has been

---

of a multitude of voters. If in such vast populations as those of the United States, France or England, there were no party organisations, by whom would public opinion be roused and educated to certain specific purposes? Each party, no doubt, tries to present its own side of the case for or against any doctrine or proposal, but the public cannot help learning something about the other side also, for even party spirit cannot separate the nation into water-tight compartments; and the most artful or prejudiced party spell-binder or newspaper has to recognise the existence of the arguments he is trying to refute. Thus party strife is a sort of education for those willing to receive instruction, and something soaks through even into the less interested or thoughtful electors. The parties keep a nation's mind alive, as the rise and fall of the sweeping tide freshens the water of long ocean inlets."—Viscount Bryce, *Modern Democracies*, Vol. I, Ch. XI, Part I, p. 134.

the emergence and maintenance of two great parties, both of which have had a certain continuity of existence from the Long Parliament down to the present time. At periods, these two parties have seemed together to comprise the active political life of the community, and it has become customary to speak of the "two-party system." The use of the term "system" conveys, perhaps, a rather misleading impression, since it suggests a formalism and rigidity which are, in fact, conspicuously absent.

At the same time, there are always powerful influences making for the maintenance of this "two-party system." Our political machinery, which has developed on the basis of two great parties, operates in that direction. The clearest illustration of that is provided by our system of single-member constituencies, in which the candidate securing more votes than any other candidate is declared elected; a system which, as we all know, does not work satisfactorily when there are more than two parties, but which operates in a highly discouraging manner to the smaller parties. It has often been suggested that even the seating arrangements in the House of Commons are not entirely without influence in this respect. More important, however, is the tradition of party government, and the political instinct (some might call it common sense) of the electors. There is a marked reluctance to vote for a party which has little chance of securing a majority of its own. The path of a third party is an arduous one, whether the third party is a new party or an old party which has fallen on evil days. The preference of the British elector for a one-party Cabinet supported by a one-party majority has often been expressed. After a period of coalition or minority government, considerable numbers of electors are willing to forgo secondary political objectives for the sake of securing relatively smooth and relatively clear government. They tend to vote for the party which, in their view, does stand a good chance of obtaining a clear majority over all others combined. More often than not their choice falls upon the party of the Right, which is rather less prone to dissensions than the party or parties of the Left.

There is a natural connection between Cabinet government and what we call the "two-party system." If our system of government is to work with the maximum degree of smoothness and efficiency, it is desirable that two conditions should be fulfilled. First, the members of the Cabinet should be drawn from the same party. Having a similar general political outlook, and usually accustomed to working together, as a consequence of their party association, they are more likely to co-operate harmoniously and effectively in the Cabinet than persons drawn from more than one party. Secondly, the majority in the popular House should be composed of members of the same party. Otherwise, there is bound to be friction between the Cabinet and the House of Commons, with resulting weakness and instability of government. The essential point is that, if harmony is to be secured between the executive government and the legislature, the Cabinet and the majority in the House of Commons must be of the same party complexion; but, if the Cabinet is to act with the maximum degree of strength and coherence, it should be a single-party Cabinet supported by a single-party majority. When such a

Cabinet resigns, it is desirable that it should be succeeded by another Cabinet of the same type—a Cabinet
composed of members of another party, also supported
by a majority in the House of Commons composed
of members of that same party. That implies two great
parties and no more.

With more than two important parties, a position
in which no party has a clear majority in the House
of Commons is bound to arise, sooner or later, and to
recur. Under the multi-party conditions prevalent
in most continental parliamentary régimes, it is
almost certain that no single party will be able
to secure a working majority. ⟨Coalition or minority
ministries are constructed, often with much difficulty
and after considerable delay. These lack as a
rule the desirable degree of unity and responsibility.
They cannot easily carry out a coherent policy
because their work has to be based to some extent
upon bargaining instead of natural political compromise. In such circumstances, ministries are relatively unstable and repeated political crises are
the result.

It is not suggested that the two-party system is
indispensable, but only that it provides the most
satisfactory conditions for the working of the Cabinet
system. The essential requirement—harmonious co-
operation between the Cabinet and the legislature—
can be secured under coalition conditions, so long
as the coalition itself is harmonious. A coalition government may be, in certain circumstances, both strong
and efficient, although that usually happens when it
is more than the solution to a situation in which no
party has a clear majority.

The two-party "system," however, has important advantages over a three-party or multi-party "system." A relatively stable parliamentary majority is, as a rule, forthcoming. Consequently, Governments normally enjoy greater security of tenure, and, therefore, better opportunities for effective action. They do not have to function in a state of more or less continuous uncertainty. Ministerial crises are relatively few, and are seldom of long duration. The change-over from one administration to another is effected with the minimum of disturbance and delay. The Opposition Party is ready to provide an alternative administration. From the standpoint of the electorate, the two-party system undoubtedly simplifies the issues and clarifies responsibility.

4. *Criticisms of the " Two-Party System "*

The simplicity of the system, however, may be regarded as deceptive. Its critics are outspoken on the point. We are told that it is a highly artificial arrangement, and that it distorts the expression of the nation's mind. The main argument employed is that "there are always more than two schools of thought in the nation."[1] It is a little difficult to define a "school of thought," but, no doubt, it is true that there are more than two of them. It does not follow, however, that each "school" should form the basis of a separate political party; nor does it follow that a party system not functioning on such a basis distorts the nation's verdict. There is no ready-made "mind" of the "nation": there are hundreds of thousands, millions, of electors with the most diverse views and the utmost

[1] Ramsay Muir, *How Britain is Governed*, p. 147.

variety of political interest and intelligence. Some kind of order has to be evolved out of this chaos, and party, as we have seen, plays an indispensable part in the process. It would, no doubt, constitute a great advance to have voters lining up in response to appeals from, say, seven parties. But why stop there? The "nation's mind" is not yet ascertained: no "national verdict" has yet been given. Only when a majority is forthcoming can there even be said to be a national verdict; only then can it be plausibly contended that the nation's mind is made up. Even then, a great deal of expert interpretation is required. But there is no justification for the presumption that the result of an appeal by two parties is any more "distorted" than that of an appeal by seven. One prominent critic of the two-party system has, indeed, asserted that a three-party system is the natural grouping in modern circumstances, but all the arguments he employs against the former apply with equal force against the latter. The ascent from two parties to three, or from three to seven, does not imply an ascent from political immorality to political virtue.

It is similar with most of the arguments used against the two-party system. They are, in fact, arguments against the abuse of the party spirit, not against the two-party position as such. Experience does not justify the assumption that parties under a multi-party system (or a three-party system) are less prone to misrepresent their opponents, to mislead the general public, to indulge in irresponsible opposition or obstruction, or to lust after power. Experience does not suggest that the smaller parties under such a system are less rigid, less doctrinaire, or more averse

from discipline. Indeed, there is a great deal to be said
for the view that the parties under a two-party system
have shown themselves less liable to some of these
defects of partisanship and bigotry. Nevertheless,
there are special dangers in a two-party system, and
realisation of these goes far to explain the criticisms to
which the system has been subjected. It *is* liable to con-
vey a false impression of simplicity. Active partisans
are not given to critical investigation of the nature of
majorities secured. The more ardent among them are
often deceived as to the true condition of their own
party membership. "It is the very snare of a large
and victorious majority, that it mistakes the volume
of its own agreement for a public verdict in its favour."
No party (under a two-party system or otherwise)
is more than an organised minority, appealing for
support to the rest of the community. Given two-party
conditions, a majority is not difficult to obtain. The
motives and reasons of those constituting the majority
are many, and may be extremely diverse. Even if
the party concerned has been a model of political
virtue in its electoral campaign, one thing is certain :
the support forthcoming never represents unqualified
support either of its general policy or of its particular
proposals. There is a real danger that this will be
inadequately appreciated by the successful party,
and it is certain not to be sufficiently recognised by an
important body of opinion within the party. Consequently, there is a danger that the party may proceed
to act in virtue of a support it does not in fact possess,
quite apart from the possibility, ever-present, of a
deliberate misuse of majority powers. Those who
determine party policy, having apparent majority

backing, and having the formal powers of a majority, may endeavour to impose their will upon the community. The development of "mandates" and "programmes", the growth of party discipline in various forms, the attempts to exercise control over parliamentary representatives, and to narrow the scope for discretionary action and leadership, may all accentuate these dangers, although, let it be noted, they themselves tend to weaken the two-party system. It is on this ground that the two-party system is most vulnerable. That it makes possible majority-tyranny seems to constitute the real gravamen of Professor Muir's criticisms of the existing system of government in this country.[1]

[1] Professor Muir's chief remedy is Proportional Representation. He emphasises the fact that it is possible, when there are more than two parties, for a party with a minority of votes to secure a majority of seats in the House of Commons under our existing electoral system. Opinions upon the wisdom of changing that system in such circumstances will largely depend upon the views held about the prospects of a return to two-party conditions. But Professor Muir, of course, does not desire such a return, and he dislikes the prospect of a party obtaining majority backing under *any* circumstances. He rightly anticipates that the introduction of Proportional Representation at this stage would prevent a return to the two-party system, and would make it difficult, though not by any means impossible, for any party to secure a majority. However, he seems to think that Proportional Representation would make it impossible for a party to exercise a "dictatorship," and that is not the case, for it would still be possible for a party to get a majority and to attempt to impose its will dictatorially. Much more important is the probability, in existing circumstances, that Proportional Representation, by preventing any party from securing a majority, would produce a deadlock and provide a dangerous stimulus to anti-parliamentary movements. On the other hand, a position in which no party has a clear majority ought not to prevent effective co-operation between the parties, and might, indeed, make its necessity more obvious. Viewing Proportional Representation solely from this standpoint (it is impossible here to examine fully the arguments for and against), its desirability or otherwise seems to be mainly dependent upon an estimate of (1) the likely behaviour of parties under Proportional Representation if it were introduced now, (2) the risk under such a system of strengthening the present-day reaction

In any event, it would be unwise to draw too sharp a distinction between a two-party system and a multi-party or group system. All kinds of political groups are bound to exist. Under a two-party system they are combined in a particular way, not eliminated. Under a multi-party system, they (or the more important of them) function separately, and are faced with the problems of combination and agreement. It is held on the one side that a two-party system conceals the real position, and therefore fails to make clear the need for seeking agreement. By making possible nominal majorities it encourages delusive hopes and rash expectations; and it results in violent oscillations of policy. The very existence of a number of parties or groups, no one of which can hope to impose its will upon the others, would compel the modification of partisanship, and the achievement of reasonable compromises. On the other side, it is contended that a multi-party system increases the opportunities for obstruction, tends to rigidity, and, in practice, increases the difficulties not only of securing the desirable measure of agreement but also of securing the indispensable measure of agreement among a majority of the community without which parliamentary government cannot function. It confuses and irritates the electorate; while the deceptive impressions of simplicity and clarity which may be engendered by the two-party system can be countered in other ways. On this side,

---

against parliamentary democracy, and (3) the dangers which might arise under the existing electoral system from a party or parties intending to utilise majority powers undemocratically or for the purpose of establishing a dictatorship. At the present time, the introduction of Proportional Representation seems more likely to endanger than to improve the working of our system of parliamentary government.

it is held that the circumstances of a two-party situation impose upon the parties concerned the requisite caution, breadth, and flexibility; and that, in fact, the oscillations of policy are not of a violent character.[1]

5. *The Breakdown of the " Two-Party System "*

Consideration of the nature of British parties under the two-party conditions which have predominated may help to elucidate the merits of these respective contentions; but it is clear that the problems of representative government are essentially the same under both sets of conditions assumed. In this respect, as in others, practical tests should be applied, and from that standpoint, the balance of advantage would seem to lie with the two-party arrangement. That, at any rate, is the verdict of British practice up-to-date; and the verdict is, on the whole, confirmed by the experience of countries under multi-party systems.

In post-war years the "breakdown" of the two-party system has been the subject of much comment. Many people regard the breakdown as final. In their opinion the tendency is towards the disintegration of the great parties, and the development of a multi-party or group system. There is a danger here of taking too short a view. In any event, it is as yet premature to assume the final disappearance of the two-party system. At the moment of writing, all parties are, to a greater or less degree, in the melting-pot; and it

[1] "The true check upon a presumptuous Government and a hasty Legislature is the existence of an alternative party, numbering its adherents by hundreds of thousands in the constituencies, and having its articulate chiefs in the House of Commons itself."—Sir Sidney Low, *The Governance of England*, p. 125.

is well within the bounds of possibility that a two-party position will re-emerge. The present transitional phase of parties is no new phenomenon in British politics, but a constantly recurring feature. It is appropriate to enquire how far the two-party "system" has been operative in this country, and to examine a little more closely what is involved in the two-party system as we have known it.

6. *A Summary of British Party Development*

An adequate history of British political parties yet remains to be written, and to attempt anything more than an indication of the main features would take us beyond the scope of this book, and beyond our powers.

The basic fact of modern British party history, undoubtedly, has been the existence of two great parties, but it was only very gradually, and with many ups and downs, that they jointly acquired a dominance over British political life. That dominance, of course, has never been immune from challenge, and it has always been contingent upon the maintenance of certain conditions.

These two parties may be traced back at least as far as the second half of the reign of Charles II, but, so far from comprising virtually all active politicians, they then represented rather factions of extremists. Throughout the reigns of James II, William III, and Anne, the decisive influence, apart from that of the monarchs themselves, was often wielded by statesmen who stood outside the political parties, although the latter were growing in strength and party strife was never more bitter. There was a large body of political opinion as yet unattached, or only very loosely associated with the parties. During this period, all ministries, whether predominantly Whig or predominantly Tory, were coalition ministries. No Cabinet was drawn exclusively from one party. That is true even of the famous Tory Ministry of 1710-1714. There was never a clean sweep of Ministers; the transition from predominantly Tory to predominantly Whig, or vice versa, was gradual. Ministries did not change because of the results of General Elections; indeed, a change of ministry frequently determined the result of the Elections. Largely due, of course, to the personal influence of the monarch and the general constitutional position, this may also be attributed to the extremism and relative weakness of the parties, and to the rudimentary nature of party organisation. Parties were groups of prominent politicians rather than popular organisations.

The accession of the House of Hanover (which produced far less extensive constitutional changes than is ordinarily supposed) checked the development of the "two-party system," however much it may have facilitated the growth of Cabinet government. The Tory Party was shattered, and Tories entirely excluded from administration. Until the new dynasty was felt to be securely established, the Whig Party dominated the situation. There was party government, but there was only one party in the running; and the eventual outcome of the disappearance of the Tory Party as an effective force was the disintegration of the Whig Party itself. Old issues were dead; new issues were being formulated; parties were, in reality, in a transitional phase. A general state of Whiggery

prevailed. Aristocratic groups of real or nominal
"Whigs" competed for royal favour and political
power.

George III's activities only intensified a process
which had already gone far. It is clear that from the
accession of George I down to the Ministry of Lord
North (1770–1782), there was nothing even approximating to a two-party system. In the constitutional
struggles of George III's reign, the issue of party
government was directly raised, the ideal of party
government proclaimed by Burke, and the two main
parties re-emerged.

The French Revolution, and the consequential wars,
led to the disruption of the revived Whig Party, and
to the long period of Tory domination from 1783 until
1830. There were still two main parties, but they did
not stand alone : there were secessions from both. The
revived Tory Party eventually suffered a similar fate
to that which befell the Whigs during their period of
domination in the early Hanoverian period. It split
into several groups ; and growing divergencies in outlook resulted finally in the important breach of 1827,
when the followers of Canning became a separate
party. Throughout this period, the main body of the
Whigs formed no more than one of a number of parties
and groups. So weak were they that they only participated in office in the brief "Ministry of All the Talents"
(1806–7), and in the short administrations of Canning
and Goderich (1827). Alone, they could not provide
an alternative Ministry ; and, indeed, it was not until
1830 that Whig unity was restored. In this period,
it is clear, the two-party system was not in working
order.

Parliamentary Reform brought the Whigs to the front of the stage once more, but it is significant that the Ministry of 1830 was "first and foremost a coalition to carry reform";[1] a coalition of Whigs, Canningites, and unattached persons. The alliance with the Canningites became permanent. On the other side, Peel revived the fortunes of the other great party, endeavouring to transform it from a Tory into a Conservative Party. Conditions once again approximated to those of a two-party system, despite the complication introduced by the Irish Party under O'Connell, especially from the General Election of 1833 until the latter's alliance with the Whigs in 1835.

This state of affairs lasted only until 1846, when the Tory-Conservative Party was split in two by the Repeal of the Corn Laws. Peel and his Free Trade colleagues constituted in fact a separate party group, which continued to exist long after Peel's death, and did not finally disappear until 1859. The years from 1846 until 1859 were a period of great party confusion, in which Lord Palmerston rose to a position of personal supremacy. It is well to recall this phase, which marks the transition from Toryism to Disraelian Conservatism, and from Whiggism to Gladstonian Liberalism. Minority government, regarded as an alarming novelty in 1924, was a feature of the period. In 1852, we had a Tory minority government under Derby and Disraeli; from 1852 to 1855, a Whig-Peelite coalition under the Peelite Earl of Aberdeen; and from 1855 to 1858 a Palmerstonian Whig adminis-tration. The year 1858 witnessed a second Tory

[1] G. M. Trevelyan, *Lord Grey of the Reform Bill*, p. 250.

F

minority government, and 1859 another Palmerstonian ministry which, including the Peelite Gladstone, paved the way for a restoration of the two-party system, definitely accomplished in 1868 after a third Tory minority government.

Yet it has been said that the Parliament of 1868–1874 "was the last in which the two-party system might be observed in perfect working order."[1] In 1874, 58 Irish Home Rulers were returned under the leadership of Isaac Butt, and the following year marked Parnell's entry into the House of Commons. The Irish Party constituted a breach of a peculiar kind in the two-party arrangement. It held the balance of power in the House of Commons in 1885–6, again in 1892–5, and from January, 1910, until the outbreak of the Great War. However, owing to the Party's alliance with one of the two great English parties after 1885, its existence did not in itself seriously disturb the working of the two-party system, although it exercised profound effects upon the course of British politics. One of its indirect consequences was the secession of the Unionists from the Liberal Party in 1886. From that year until 1895, the Liberal-Unionists formed a separate group in Parliament. They worked however, in a close alliance with the Conservative Party which quickly developed into a merger.

The General Election of 1906 marked the effective entry of an independent Labour Party into the House of Commons, but, until the Great War, it constituted little more than the Left Wing of the Liberal Party. It may be held, therefore, that there was for all practical

[1] May's *Constitutional History of England*, Vol. III, (Francis Holland), p. 76.

purposes a two-party system in this country from 1859 until the War of 1914, despite the existence of the Irish Party and the advent of the Labour Party. The War brought about the elimination of the Irish Party, but, by seriously weakening the Liberal Party, and facilitating the rise of the Labour Party, it produced a clear breakdown of the two-party arrangement.

7. Some Conclusions

Certain conclusions may be drawn from this brief summary of British party history. The present party confusion is not unique: the two-party system did not break down for the first time during the War of 1914–18. The main feature of our party life has been the existence of two great parties, but this has not meant, as a rule, two parties only. Looking at the whole course of development, we have seldom had a position in which there were two parties and no more. At the same time, had it not been for the "foreign" element provided by the Irish Party, there would have been a clear two-party position from 1859 until 1906, save for the temporary existence of the Liberal Unionist Group from 1886 until 1895. As a rule, however, there have been more than two parties. And we may note, in particular, the succession of break-aways by centrist groups, such as the Canningites, the Peelites, the Liberal Unionists, and, to give another example, the followers of Mr. Lloyd George in 1916. The followers of Mr. MacDonald, separated from the rest of the Labour Party owing to the events of 1931, constitute only the latest illustration of a split in the ranks of one of the two great parties.

Apart from breakaways towards the centre, there has been the emergence of new groups or parties, either on the Right or on the Left of the two main parties, or on some special issue. The Irish Nationalist Party, and, later, Sinn Fein, provide instances of the latter: they were, in fact, foreign elements in the body politic. More important was the emergence of the Labour Party, and its rise after the War to a position in which it overshadowed one of the two great historic parties. The Labour Party is by no means the first or the last example of the emergence of a new group on the Left. It provided, however, the first instance of such a group developing into a strong separate party. It succeeded in doing what the Radical groups or "parties" of the nineteenth century were never able to accomplish. Similarly, there have been groups on the extreme Right, though no new Party has as yet arisen. The possibility, however, exists.

It is important to note, therefore, that there is nothing in the "two-party system" to prevent the emergence of a new party. The possibility of this happening is, in a sense, a condition of the continuance of the two-party system. The potential or actual rise of a new party compels the adaptation, either of the two existing parties, or of the party system as a whole, to new political forces and circumstances. A new political group need not organise itself into a party, for its aims may be more effectively promoted from within one of the existing combinations. Much will depend upon the attitude of the existing parties towards it, and the possibility of the formation of a new party will have its effect upon their behaviour. If a new party definitely emerges, it will usually be the result of a lack of adaptibility displayed by one or other or both of the two previously existing parties. In that event, there will be a temporary breakdown of the two-party system.

It does not follow, however, from the actual formation of a new party that the breakdown will be more than temporary. The rigidity which led to its formation may be broken down by its formation. Eventually, the new party may be merged in one or other of the two great parties. Alternatively, it may grow in strength, gaining adherents from one or both of the two great parties, until it emerges as one of the two great parties, the remaining elements in the two former parties merging into one great opposing party. The phenomenal rise of the Labour Party provides clear evidence of the fact that it is not impossible for a third party itself to rise to power and to become one of the two great parties in the State. However, it may be suggested that the rise of the Labour Party would not have taken place had the Liberal Party at the time been more receptive of the ideas and policies advanced by the early Labour people. More important still, the Labour Party would not have grown so rapidly in strength had not the Liberal Party broken up as a consequence of the Great War.

Despite the breakaways that have occurred, and the emergence of new parties, the conclusion is warranted that there has been a strong tendency towards restoration of two-party conditions. The difficult situation of the Peelites has been adequately portrayed by Gladstone's biographer. They were only able to hold out longer as an independent political force than, say, the Liberal Unionists, because of the

general political conditions then obtaining. The
extension of the franchise and the growth of party
organisation, in conjunction with the nature of our
electoral system, has made the position of small
parties much more difficult. The Liberal Unionists
can hardly be said ever to have formed a separate
and independent political party. Chamberlain has
left on record an account of his relations with the
parties from 1888 to 1892 which illuminates the
difficulties of a seceding and intermediate group.[1]
There is strong ground for contending that, in the days
before the War, the Labour Party was merging into
the Liberal Party. It is significant that Mr. Mac-
Donald, in discussing this question in 1909, viewed
the possibility of eventual merger with apparent
equanimity.[2] Since the war, the Liberal Party, holding
a relatively weak intermediate position, has tended to
disintegrate. There were movements away from it
in both directions, and the tendency was towards the
absorption of the Party, partly into the Conservative
Party, and partly into the Labour Party. In so far
as the Liberal Party remained, the sections into which
it had been divided by the War tended to coalesce,
and, indeed, effective unity had been achieved for some
time before the political crisis of 1931 began to
develop.

That crisis, of course, brought about a new and
confused party situation. It remains to be seen

[1] J. L. Garvin, *Life of Joseph Chamberlain*, Vol. II, pp. 413–6.
[2] *Socialism and Government*, Vol. II, p. 19.—". . . the application of what is written in this section is not that the Labour Party
should cease to exist, but that it should go on assimilating until
it becomes one of the two great parties, or its principles and objects
have become those of one of the two great parties."

whether a new two-party arrangement will eventually emerge. Much will depend upon the attitude taken up by the existing parties and groups, and especially upon the behaviour of the Labour Party, which still has it in its power to become one of the two great parties under a two-party system. In short, it depends upon whether or not British parties are going to retain the characteristics and habits acquired by them *pari passu* with the development of our system of government.

CHAPTER III

1. *Class or National Parties?*

WHAT has been the real basis of division between the two main English parties? What are the bonds of union which have produced and maintained them respectively?

Some writers, influenced by Marxism, profess to find the answers to these questions in economic class-interest. This view has been expressed, for instance, by Mr. A. L. Rowse, in his *Politics and the Younger Generation*.

"A party is at bottom a complex of group-interests; it may have also an historical tradition and a programme. . . . All the parties are class-parties: they represent an agglomeration of class-interests, and if you seek the motive-force of their policy you must look to their centre of gravity which is in some class."

Parties, it is urged, express the existing social conditions, in which economic factors are the determinants. Men are not divided by conflicting views, or united by similar views, of what is for the community's well-being, though they may think they are. Indeed, men are not united and divided on any rational or moral grounds at all, but by similar or conflicting individual and group and class interests. These latter constitute the realities of politics: all the rest is smoke-screen. Political parties are, in fact, based upon economic classes, and it is desirable that this basis should be frankly recognised. The moral appeal in politics may just as well be abandoned; it is futile, even if not actually irrelevant.

It is not possible here adequately to examine this view and its implications. There are certain difficulties of interpretation. It is one thing to say that a party is a complex of economic groups or classes, and another to say that a party is an economic class, or is based upon an economic class; that it is a class-party. How are the groups or classes combined into "a class?" What is the basis of union? The class structure of society is, admittedly, complex and changing. Mr. Rowse emphasises its "subtlety and complexity." The analysis which divides the community into two classes, e.g. the "possessing class" and the "working class," is clearly inadequate and misleading. Yet Mr. Rowse, dealing with the position as it existed before the political crisis of 1931, insists that "below the surface where there are three parties, there is in fact only one cleavage, and you are on either one side or the other," and he writes of the possessing classes on the one side, and the working classes on the other.

Obviously, this has not been the basis of party division in the past; and it is equally clear that it is not its basis in the present. Even on the assumption that parties have always been based upon economic class-interests, it is apparent that the class-interests respectively represented by the two British parties have varied from time to time. We are still left, therefore, with the problem of the basis of alignment into two parties.

That there is a considerable amount of truth in this kind of view will readily be granted. It is true that all parties have at all times represented to some extent special class or group interests. It is true, in particular, that sectional interests of one kind or another are increasingly powerful in the modern world owing to their high standard of organisation, and seek to use one party or another in pursuit of their sectional aims and interests. It is not true, however, that the great British parties have been or are class parties. That is to say, they have not been, and are not, composed exclusively of people drawn from one class or group of classes ; and they have not pursued, and do not pursue, policies based exclusively upon the interests of any one class or group of classes.

Indeed, in so far as any British party tends to develop into a party of that kind it loses strength. A British party has to make a wider appeal. At the very lowest, its class or sectional aims have to be subordinated, in practice, to a policy which can be effectually represented as being in the interests of the community as a whole. The Labour Party, for instance, at one time appealed almost exclusively to the manual workers ; and it still draws its main strength from the Trade Unions. But it contained from the beginning people who approved the Party's aims, regardless of their own class or sectional or personal interests. It is worth recalling, also, that the Labour Party met with no great measure of success until it opened its doors wide to all men and women, irrespective of class or economic status, who were prepared to support its policy. Even so, the Labour Party has suffered in the public estimation, justly or unjustly, because of the measure of control, rightly or wrongly estimated, exercised over it by the Trade Unions. Similarly, the Conservative Party (and, to some extent, the Liberal Party also) has suffered from its subservience, real or alleged, to particular "vested interests."

Moreover, while it is the case that economic forces exercise a powerful influence in politics, here as elsewhere, they are by no means the only forces operative. Many people may be primarily concerned about their own economic interests, whether personal, family, sectional or class, but all people are not by any means exclusively concerned with them. This view implies that the members of the community are incapable of pursuing any common purpose; which is not the case. Moral forces may be relatively weak, but they are operative, and cannot wisely be ignored. Furthermore, even if people were animated solely by economic motives, the result would not be a clear-cut division between "the possessing classes" and "the working classes." The development of Fascism in its various forms has finally exploded that notion. Economic interest does not range men into a neatly ordered series of classes capable of being combined for party purposes in that kind of way. In this matter, appeal is made to the facts, and the facts are clear and conclusive.

No British party has been a class party either in composition or policy. Each has drawn a measure of support from all groups and classes in the community. It has been pointed out[1]—on the implied assumption that the Conservative Party stands for the

[1] H. Finer, *The Theory and Practice of Modern Government*, Vol. I, pp. 527–8.

defence of the propertied classes—that the figures of voting themselves show that over one-half the followers of Conservatism have no direct economic interest in the success of the party. Mr. Rowse has perforce to admit the fact that "both Conservatives and Liberals possess a considerable working-class vote." He asserts that the tendency is for these elements to gravitate to the Labour Party. It remains to be seen whether or not his judgment is sound, but, whatever may happen in the future, his description of the parties does not as yet conform to the realities of the situation. The very argument that if only people were class-conscious the party situation would be other than it is, constitutes an admission that parties are not yet class-parties.[1] What is really contended by those who take this kind of view is not so much that parties are class-parties as that they ought to be; not that people do look primarily to the economic interests of their group, but that they ought so to look. So far as the parties we have known in this country are concerned, their explanation must be rejected as inadequate; and there seems no likelihood that it will become adequate in the future.

2. *The Nature of British Parties under the " Two-Party System "*

Before attempting to provide a more satisfactory explanation, it is desirable to consider more fully the nature of British parties as they have existed under the two-party conditions which, on the whole, have

[1] Mr. Rowse laments that "the working class . . . is least of all conscious of its interests."

prevailed in the past. There are some elementary but all too prevalent misunderstandings.

While there is a certain type of person who professes to see no greater difference between the political parties than that between Tweedledum and Tweedledee, the party man is very apt to exaggerate the differences. Normally, a party is credited with far too distinctive and homogeneous a character. Politically, a Conservative is regarded as a person totally different from a Liberal, and a Labour man is assumed to have nothing in common politically with a Tory. Not only so, but all Conservatives are thought of as quite different from all Liberals, and no Labour man is thought to have anything personal in common with any Conservative. It is assumed that a Conservative, a Liberal, or a member of the Labour Party, has certain definite and clearly distinguishable political views, or, at least, is animated by certain definite political motives. Everyone knows that these things are not so, but most people speak and act as though they were, except, of course, when they are busy pointing out what a hopelessly mixed and disunited lot their opponents are.

The actual position is that the members of the community cannot be arranged politically into two, or even into a dozen, clearly defined blocks. It is not even possible to arrange political opinions or interests into an ordered series of gradations stretching from the extreme Right to the extreme Left. Such gradations, shading imperceptibly into one another, are complicated and broken up by innumerable cross-currents related to particular issues. The structure of political opinion and interest is extremely complex, loose and variable. That is always the case. If there are two main parties, therefore, they must of necessity be broad, comprehensive parties, embracing all kinds and conditions of people, with diverse views, interests, and degrees of political intelligence and public spirit.

It is true that in politics we are not concerned merely with individuals. The latter, particularly in modern times, are organised in many different ways: there is a great variety of political groupings. British parties, therefore, have always comprised a number of groups. Their aim has been to secure the support of a majority of the electorate, and thus to assume responsibility for the government of the community. Consequently, the basis and appeal of any such party must be broadly national. A British party is composite, not homogeneous. It cannot be a sectional party, representing merely some one interest or group of interests, or one class or group of classes. Nor can a British party be doctrinaire and dogmatic. It cannot safely impose doctrinal tests; it cannot be a select body of the righteous, a party of zealots. Its practical policy cannot safely be narrow; for its objective is to secure control of the whole government of the country, not to carry some one measure or set of measures.[1] In short, a Party such as we have been accustomed to must be wide, tolerant of internal differences, elastic, and adaptable to changing circumstances.

Numerous illustrations might be given of the composite nature of British parties, but one has only to enquire into the parliamentary personnel at any given period, or even into the personnel of any Cabinet. Consider Gladstone's Cabinet of 1880, with its Whigs,

[1] See Amos, p. 72, *op. cit.*

its Liberals, and its Radicals old and new. When the Unionists among them seceded in 1886, they were not themselves by any means a united body; they comprised at least two groups. Or examine the personnel of the Labour Party to-day, with its Trade Unionists, Socialists of every conceivable variety, Radical Nonconformists, Catholic working-men, Liberal Pacifists, Democrats and Revolutionaries. The truth is that every British party has been and is a coalition of groups. The point is important in several connections. It helps, for instance, to counteract the customary exaggeration of the difference between a single-party Ministry and a coalition Ministry. A Coalition Government is a coalition of parties or groups. A "Party" Government represents a coalition of groups. The difference is one of degree, not of kind. It may happen, indeed, that a coalition ministry is more homogeneous than some single-party ministries : it would be unwise to assume the contrary.

It follows that the boundary line between the two main parties is vague and indeterminate. They shade imperceptibly into one another. There may be clear-cut opposition on some particular issue, but there never has been a clear-cut opposition all along the line. Few are the concrete and particular questions upon which some party members as well as party supporters do not agree with their opponents rather than with their colleagues. More often than not, there is more in common between the Left Wing Conservative and the Right Wing Liberal or Labour man, than there is between either of them and their respective extremists. Furthermore, it may be suggested that there is usually more in common between the relatively intelligent and experienced on both sides than between them and their party colleagues. There is no gulf, therefore, fixed between the parties; and, since there is no gulf to be bridged, transition from one to the other is easy. Harder, of course, for active party members than for ordinary party supporters, and hardest of all for leaders, it is not too difficult even for these.

Another necessary consequence of the history and nature of our political parties is that they have not each represented an unchanging, stereotyped, policy. It follows from the mere fact of their continuity that they have constantly adapted their policies and pro-grammes to new situations; that they have undergone a never-ceasing process of change and development. Even their names have undergone some adaptation. It follows also, from the great economic and social changes that have taken place, and from the pro-gressive extension of the franchise, as well as from the course of political struggles, that the component elements of the parties have varied from time to time.

A superficial glance at the policies pursued might suggest the conclusion that the parties have had no permanent basis; that they have been mere bottles continually refilled with any mixture which happened to be handy at the time. The history of each party conveys the impression of a maze of inconsistencies and contradictions. A closer examination, however, would show, as is so often the case in politics, that the contradictions are more apparent than real, and the inconsistencies secondary, arising in the main from changes of circumstances.

Sir Sidney Low has written that "it is a difficult, perhaps even an impossible, task to draw a dividing line from age to age between the two parties, on the basis of doctrine."[1] That is true, and it is only to be expected. Nevertheless there is something permanent in the Party of the Right, something common to it through all its vicissitudes of policy and fortune, something which links the Conservative of to-day with the Tory of 1832, with the Tory of the reign of Queen Anne, and even with the Cavalier of the Restoration Parliament, something which has required differing interpretations at different times. The same is true of the Party of the Left, though here, perhaps, the common element is less easily discernible.[2]

3. "Conservatism" and "Progress"

What, then, are the respective common elements? It is here suggested that the real basis of division between the parties has been between those who stand, on the whole, for the maintenance of the existing ways of life, and those who stand, on the whole, for changes which are regarded by them as "progressive."[3]

[1] The Governance of England, p. 127.

[2] "Even as political feeling and thought produce variety of doctrine and behaviour according to place, so do they according to time, and the history of Conservative and Liberal doctrines is necessarily one of digressions and deviations from their central character: but the central character is there, it does determine the solution in time and place, and, moreover, it is peculiar and clearly distinguishable."—H. Finer, Vol. I, pp. 515–6, op. cit.

[3] "There are two principal powers in politics. One is the great wish of all ordinary decent people, poor and rich, to lead the life to which they have been used, and to think the thoughts to which they have been accustomed. . . . On the other hand, there is in States a mighty innovating—it would almost be clearer to say, revolutionary impulse."—Bagehot, The Chances for a long Conservative Régime in England.

"Men have always been, and must be, drawn into camps of progress and of caution."—Lord Courtney, The Working Constitution of the United Kingdom, p. 138.

G

It is the old explanation, and it seems the only one that fits the facts. There are two main attitudes of mind, which may or may not be strengthened (they usually are) by considerations of economic interest. There are those who are, on the whole, conservatively-minded, and those who are, on the whole, progressively-minded. This rather vague division, it is suggested, has its counterpart in the alignment into two great parties, the Party of the Right and the Party of the Left, whatever their actual names may be at any given time.

It should be remembered, however, that there is no clear-cut distinction between the conservative spirit and the progressive spirit. The two are not incompatible, and, therefore, as Benedetto Croce has reminded us, they cannot be given "material form as two different and opposing programmes." The programme of the one party is never entirely unprogressive; the programme of the other is never entirely unconservative. Indeed, it may happen that in certain spheres and in particular periods, the Party of the Right may be more progressive than the Party of the Left.[1] Moreover, the conservative and progressive tendencies co-exist in most individuals, if not in all, though in varying proportions. It is a question only of degree.

The contention that conservatism and progress

[1] "Caution and progressiveness are only two of the characteristics which all or most men possess in greater or less degree. In private life, and in ordinary relations, it would be no easier to range them into these two classes than under any other equally comprehensive categories. And it is impossible to maintain that these attributes have been constant in the two great English parties. The Conservatives or Tories have often been progressive; the Liberals or Whigs stationary or retrogressive."—Low, *op. cit.*, p. 126.

have provided the basis of party division is, at least, not incompatible with the known facts of British party history. It helps to explain the indeterminate nature of the boundary between the parties.

Certain supplementary points call for mention. Not only may a conservative temperament be combined with desire for change, and a sanguine temperament with opposition to change, but party affiliations may be determined or influenced by the accidents of early associations, family traditions, and social environment. Party allegiance is, in a large number of cases, traditional; and it is very frequently blind. "My party, right or wrong" is as often the unconscious basis of domestic political action as "My country, right or wrong" is of action in regard to international affairs. Many an elector in this country is Conservative, Liberal or Labour, much in the same way as he backs Cambridge for the Boat Race, Yorkshire at cricket or the Arsenal in the Football League. A distinction must also be drawn between the avowed partisan and the occasional supporter; and yet another between those who think for themselves and those who merely follow the lead of others. Those who are normally indifferent to politics must never be overlooked.

4. *The Importance of the "Centre"*

It is clear from the nature of our party system that those who occupy a central position, unable to commit themselves whole-heartedly or for long to either the one party or the other, must be numerous and influential. Bagehot has written, with his customary insight, of—

"the great neutral mass, which is not violently in favour either of one side in politics or of the other; which inclines now more in one direction, and now more in the other; which is often nominally divided between Left and Right, between the movement and the non-movement parties, and which then forms a certain 'common element,' of which both parties partake, and the members of which are much more akin and much more like to the members of it in the other party, than they are to the extreme partisans in their own."

Mr. Keith Feiling has also suggested that this middle bloc is, perhaps, the largest, comprising as it does

"those notorious pendulum-swingers whose weight strikes the hour in tune with the earlier and sensitive note of their leaders. For leaders they have; and the history of England is made, if we are candid, much less by the Shaftesburys and Walpoles, Salisburys and Harcourts, than by a Halifax or a Godolphin, the Trimmers, Peelites and Mugwumps, who cannot help seeing both sides of a question, and commonly delay decision till all is saved, save honour."[1]

These centrist elements, be it noted, are to be found inside both the main parties, as well as among their occasional supporters,—quite apart from any intermediate party or group which may exist at any particular time. They exercise an extremely important moderating influence in both parties, and they often determine changes in party fortunes by transferring their support from the one party to the other on some particular issue, or in view of some new general tendency.

[1] *Sketches in Nineteenth Century Biography*, p. 178.

In this connection, Croce's words should be borne in mind :—

"There is no power which can prevent men from agreeing and disagreeing, not in the terms of abstract and empty programmes, but on concrete questions and practical expedients, nor from following those leaders who at various times give them hope of realizing that which seems to them to be good and desirable."[1]

Party officials, and ardent partisans generally, are apt to view moderation as treasonable, and to be scathingly contemptuous of the "pendulum-swingers"; at any rate, after electoral defeats. After victories, they are more inclined to harp on the solid common-sense of the British electors. Defeat, however, is customarily attributed to the behaviour of "the least solid, the least instructed, and the most wavering part of the electorate"—"those who can be driven this way or that by sudden panics, or electioneering 'stunts,' or campaigns of creeping slander, or wild and reckless promises."[2] The "pendulum-swingers," no doubt, include a considerable proportion of political defectives, but they are not by any means all of that kind. On the contrary, they comprise a large body of moderates whose standard of political intelligence compares favourably with that of the solid bodies of partisans, and who are inclined to be sceptical of the enthusiasms, and critical of

[1] *A History of Italy*, 1871–1914.
[2] Ramsay Muir, *op. cit.*, pp. 161–2. The writer proceeds:—"In almost any constituency a swing of perhaps 5 per cent. of the electorate—often consisting of people who have never taken any serious interest in politics, and have perhaps not even attended the meetings of the rival candidates—will give victory to one side or another."

the prejudices, which sway the latter.[1] It is a mistake
to assume that the "My party, right or wrong" man is
better instructed than the "pendulum-swinger," or
less susceptible to panic. People often talk as though
a transfer of support or of party allegiance (from
their party, of course, not vice versa) is conclusive
evidence of C3 citizenship; which is simply not the
case.

5. *The Party of the Right*

Our interpretation of the nature of British political
parties is confirmed by the facts of British political
development.

The Party of the Right (Tory or Conservative) has
been (up to the present, at any rate) conservative;
neither reactionary nor even stationary. It has had
its reactionary moments, and even periods, but they
have led to party disasters; and the lessons taught
have not been lost upon its leaders, even if they have
all too frequently been forgotten by the rank-and-
file.

Its great leaders have been men whose conservatism
"consisted less in maintaining fixed institutions than
in acting in tune with the conservative spirit."[2] Even
the more rigid of them have nearly always (if
not quite always) recognised and accepted accomplished facts. Wellington, a leader of this type, knew
when compromise was necessary, and when he had

---

[1] "The number of children born alive who defy Gilbert's law is
really very considerable; and in a country where political arrangement is much older than economic regimentation, thousands will
continue to surprise the best laid schemes of party organisers."—
Keith Feiling, *op. cit.*, p. 178.

[2] Feiling, p. 89, *op. cit.*

to give in. In any event, "the King's Government must be carried on." The greater leaders of the party have all been reformers. Oftentimes they have proposed and carried out reforms which their "progressive" opponents, for the most part, regarded at the time as undesirable or premature. They have "often done radical things from inside the conservative frame and were ceaselessly attacked by their followers in consequence." Occasionally, they have failed to carry their party supporters with them, as Peel failed in 1846. Sooner or later, however, the "Die-Hards" or "Ultras" have been reconciled. It would be putting their attitude on the lowest plane to assert that the majority of rank-and-file Tories or Conservatives in this country have consented to concessions—with grumbling and gloomy foreboding—when it has become clear to them that that was the best way of avoiding or postponing more drastic concessions. In fact, the influence of the centrist elements in the Party of the Right has always been considerable, and in the long run decisive. The Moderate Conservatives have, on the whole, controlled the policy of the Party. Bagehot summed up the situation in his masterly manner :—

"The most extreme Conservative is usually aware that some change must be carried sometimes, and he is disposed to think that perhaps the changes that his own friends incline to may be those changes. At any rate, he does not see where he can get so little change. If he leave the alliance of the Moderate Conservative, he must either stand alone, which is impotence, or ally himself with Liberals, which is hateful. For one who wants to change nothing, to combine with those who want to change more, against those who wish to change less, is ridiculous. Accordingly, the Moderate Conservatives have almost always a game at their disposal, if they are wise enough to perceive it. All that they concede, the attacking force will accept, and whatever they choose to concede, the rest of the defending force must allow."

6. *The Party of the Left*

In a similar way, the Party of the Left (Whig or Liberal or Labour) has (up to the present) never attempted to carry out a revolutionary policy, i.e. a policy involving an immediate and radical break in the continuity of social life. It has taken the view (which it will be contended is sound) that revolutionary measures and policies lead inevitably to revolutionary situations, if persisted in, and to reaction even if attempted. Its policy has been to propose and to carry separate projects each of which could be defended on its merits, and not merely by reference to any abstract principle or ideal political system or ideal social order; aiming at achieving its ideals (whatever they might be at any particular time) as a result of the cumulative effect of separate practical measures, and keeping the social life of the community functioning as smoothly as possible all the time.

Here again, leaders have not always been successful in carrying their party supporters with them, and the Party has suffered set-backs in consequence. But, on the whole, the moderate centrist elements, though less happily situated than similar elements in the other great party, have exercised effective influence. They have kept the Party of the Left on the rails of parliamentary government, for, as Bagehot put it (and he called himself a man of the Left Centre), "the Left Centre will neither drive so slow as to miss the train, or so fast as to meet with an accident."[1] In general, the conduct of the Party has been marked by a sufficient recognition of the strength of conservative sentiment and of the dangers attendant upon extremist innovations; and by a common-sense preference for half-a-loaf to no bread at all.

7. *The Reciprocal Activities of the Parties*

Where there are two great parties, the minority, sooner or later, becomes the majority, or, to be more precise, the other minority succeeds its rival in the enjoyment of majority backing. There is an alternation of the two parties in power, though a change does not necessarily take place at each appeal to the electorate. This alternation provides a salutary check upon the abuse of majority powers. Each party soon learns from experience that it cannot hope successfully to ride roughshod over the other. That lesson was painfully enforced during the later Stuart period upon the leaders of the two historic parties. It has to be learned by any new party which acquires or hopes to acquire majority powers, and the rank-and-file

[1] "In short, the Left Centre wants to introduce tested innovations when the average man begins to comprehend them, and not before; and to introduce them in the shape in which he comprehends them, and not in any other shape. If the predominant power is in the hands of men like this, they secure the State against the worst evils of Conservatism, and the worst evils of innovation. They will not allow evils to stand so long unredressed, that at last it is of little use redressing them; they will not permit new men rashly, and on a sudden, to apply new ideas which match nothing in the present world, which join on to nothing, and which mar everything."

members of each party are constantly in need of reminder about it. Both parties, even assuming their internal cohesion, have to temper their party zeal to the requirements of the situation.

It is significant, in this connection, to note that the effects of great political influences and movements have not been confined to one party. "The spirit of the age," whatever its nature might be, has permeated both. In the early part of the nineteenth century, economic liberalism found a warmer welcome in the ranks of the Tory Party than amongst the Whigs; and the era of administrative and legal reform inspired so largely by Bentham was inaugurated under the "reactionary" government of Lord Liverpool. So, in the last quarter of the nineteenth century, the movement away from "laissez faire" was participated in by both parties. Fabianism, like Benthamism before it, left its mark on Conservatives as well as Liberals. It is sometimes said that Conservatives will probably play a greater part in introducing socialistic legislation than Socialists themselves; and, if that happens, it will be in full accord with British political practice in the past.

Macaulay likened the relations between the two parties to those between the fore and hind feet of a stag, both equally necessary, and the hind feet arriving at the place where the fore feet had been. The image is defective, for it is not sufficient to say with Macaulay that "the absolute position of the parties has been altered; the relative position remains unchanged." In fact, as Sir Sidney Low has pointed out, both parties have passed and repassed one another. Nevertheless, Macaulay's remark draws attention to one important aspect of the truth, namely, that both parties have moved in the same direction, even if at differing speeds and with detours which have sometimes led them into strange places.

It is safe to say that in no department of political activity has the work been done by one party alone. Many people see, or profess to see, in politics little more than a party "dog-fight." That aspect of the matter certainly looms too large in the public view. But the fact of co-operation, less dramatic in its appeal, is normally taken for granted or ignored. The real import of the party struggle is itself unappreciated. It is out of the dialectical contention of parties that agreement and co-operation emerge. The conflict is both natural and indispensable; so also is the process of collaboration. That collaboration is partial, and often provisional; necessarily, agreement is never complete or final. The political process resulting from the contention of parties under conditions of free discussion consists essentially of a continuous series of compromises, each of which has behind it a wide measure of consent, and is, sooner or later, generally accepted, thus providing the basis for a further stage of party controversy.

Without a large measure of co-operation our system of government cannot function; without it, even the day-to-day work of Parliament cannot be carried on. If Oppositions had always adhered strictly to their alleged duty of opposition, British history would have been very different from what it has been. Sir Robert Peel's policy "in Opposition," from the passing of the Reform Act in 1832 until 1841, provides an instructive study of the spirit in which our political institutions have been operated. His acceptance of the Reform Act, his attitude, varying from benevolent neutrality to conditional support of the Whig administrations of the period, his control of the extremists of his party, are typical of the best British statesmanship.

It should be remembered that, however wide party divergencies may be at any given period, there are always important issues which cut across them, and there is always an extensive field of political action largely untouched by them. There are matters upon which those experienced in government, in and out of office, are naturally in agreement over against those of both parties who are deficient in experience or limited in a sense of responsibility.

But, however keen and prolonged the struggle between parties on a particular issue, it has repeatedly happened in British history that the final solution (if that term may legitimately be used) has been, in large measure, an agreed one. The agreements have been of varying degrees of completeness, and have taken many different forms. It may justly be said that the greatest legislative enactments of the nineteenth and twentieth centuries have been carried by the co-operation of both parties. Sometimes it has been co-operation between the party leaders : sometimes it has been the result of pressure operating through both parties upon their respective leaders. Catholic Emancipation in 1829, the Poor Law Amendment Act of 1834, the Municipal Corporations Act of the same year, the Repeal of the Corn Laws in 1846, the second Reform Bill in 1867, the Government of India Act of 1918, the Representation of the People Act of the same year, provide some instances of this kind of co-operation. The case of Irish self-government provides, perhaps, the most outstanding example of failure to achieve the necessary co-operation: it is the exception that proves the rule; and, eventually, the long-delayed solution in the Treaty of 1921 was, in this country, generally accepted. It must be noted also that co-operation between the leaders has some-times been effected at the cost of a breach in one of the parties, as in 1829, 1846, 1915–16, and 1931.

Where legislation has not been carried by fairly general agreement between the parties, or between one party and the leaders of the other, it has, as a rule, been carried by one party in such a way as to secure the acquiescence of the other party and of the community as a whole. The legislation carried by party majorities in Parliament has always been, in greater or less degree, the result of compromise, because of the need for conciliating all sections of the party in power and of its supporters in the country, and also because of the need for securing the peaceful and voluntary acquiescence of its opponents.

Legislation which provokes resistance is obviously insecure: it creates problems which are better avoided. Legislation which is so unpalatable to the opposition that its reversal at the first opportunity is certain is also insecure. Neglect of the possibility of resistance or even of repeal weakens legislative authority. British parties, on the whole, have preferred steady but permanent gains to dramatic but fleeting successes, and political continuity to political vacillation. With parties alternating in office, sudden breaks in public policy would be, clearly enough, highly disturbing, and, eventually, fatal to the system of government itself. We find, therefore, that repeal of the major measures of one government by its successor is a rare occurrence in the course of our political history up to date. Revision there has often been, simple repeal seldom if ever. Lord Salisbury stated the position very clearly :—

"What is known as 'the pendulum' has established itself as the law of English politics, and I think that within certain reasonable limits each party should accept the work of its predecessor and try, as far as it can do consistently with the public interest, to work it out to a satisfactory conclusion. And I do not think that in doing so we can be exposed to the imputation of inconsistency or of having changed our opinions."[1]

Only in this way, we suggest, can peaceful progress be made. This method is, indeed, the secret of the orderly nature of British political development. Clearly, it involves superficial and secondary inconsistencies, but, as it has been said, "stupidity in its nature is more consistent than intelligence." The glib charges of inconsistency and worse so frequently made arise essentially from lack of understanding. It is true that parties, by their own behaviour, are themselves partly responsible for them. They exaggerate their differences; they condemn too rashly; they make ill-considered promises; and they lead their supporters and the general public to expect too drastic and definite departures in policy. At the same time, it is only just to point out that these partisan faults can be imputed with less justice to leaders than to persons without

[1] Quoted by Sir Sidney Low, *The Governance of England*, p. 132.

responsibility. Unfortunately, the warnings of leaders in these matters are all too frequently ignored. Mr. MacDonald's utterances and writings during his period of leadership of the Labour Party, especially on taking office in 1924, and again in 1929, may be contrasted with the behaviour of the bulk of his party membership, and their reactions to the policies of his Ministries.

The pursuit of the methods outlined explains much in British political history which is otherwise confusing. Agreed legislation, legislative and executive action based upon moderation and compromise, rough continuity in public policy, go far to explain the fact that both parties have contributed to every important aspect of our political development. Both have played their part in the successive extensions of the franchise, in education, in factory and social legislation, in the promotion of self-government within the Empire, in financial and fiscal policy, in economic liberalism, and, subsequently, in the modern extension of the functions of the State. It is, indeed, anything but an easy task to disentangle and assess their respective contributions, and both are able to present a strong historical case for support on the basis of progressive achievement in the past.

8. *Internal Contentions and Leadership*

The course of political development has been influenced not merely by the reciprocal action of the parties themselves, but also, as has been indicated, by the interplay of personalities and groups within the respective parties. The political struggle is waged inside as well as between the parties, and in this respect, the relations of leaders with their parties have been of the first importance.

One interesting feature of the normal working of our great political parties is that the leaders of the Party of the Right are invariably denounced from their Right for betraying the interests of the nation by a policy of concession to the clamour of their opponents; while the leaders of the Party of the Left are repeatedly denounced from their Left for betraying their ideals by a policy of compromise with existing evils. Numerous illustrations might be drawn from recent events, but it is no new phenomenon. What Mr. Baldwin has to endure from his "Die-Hards" is the same sort of thing that Peel, Disraeli, Canning, even Pitt, had to contend against. Mr. MacDonald, Sir Herbert Samuel, Mr. Henderson, and even Mr. Lansbury, have to face the same criticism, and the same incipient or actual revolt from their rank-and-file as Grey, Melbourne, Russell, Gladstone and Asquith had to face. To the extreme Conservative, Mr. Baldwin appears to be at heart a Socialist. Mr. MacDonald was always regarded by his extremists as little better than a Conservative. So, to some extent, it has always been, and so it probably will be, as long as our system of government continues to function.

Such criticisms of the leaders are not a mere display of political fanaticism or malice. Behind the exaggerations of the extremists on both sides, there is a solid kernel of truth. Quite apart from the differences bound to exist between the responsible and the relatively irresponsible, it is a natural consequence of the structure of British parties, and their relations with each other and the community as a whole, that party

leaders should gravitate towards the centre. There is
much in the suggestion that, under British conditions,
no Centre Party could form a government, but all
governments must be Governments of the Centre.
The successful leader of the party of the Right must
be nearer to the Left than to the Right of his party;
while the successful leader of the Party of the Left
must be nearer to the Right than to the Left of his
party. The long-run movement in politics is towards
the Left. The leadership of the Conservative Party
moves leftwards also, to ease the strain, and to maintain the measure of unity and continuity upon which
political order depends. The successive leaders of the
progressive Party tend to move rightwards for the
same reasons, and under the same impulses. This,
and neither the alleged stupidity of the Party of the
Right, nor the alleged baseness of the leaders of the
other party, is the real explanation of the fact that the
leaders of Conservatism have often been drawn from
the other side. Mr. Feiling has remarked that "it can
hardly be accident that Harley and Bolingbroke were
of Whig descent, that the Pitts and Burke were the
same, that Derby was a Whig convert, that Disraeli
and Chamberlain began as radical reformers."[1]

It has been said of democracy, and it can assuredly
be said of British parliamentary government, that it
"means very often nothing else than opposing one's
friends for the benefit of the opponent and the welfare
of the whole." That is a point at which the parliamentary statesman comes in. Leadership into the
paths of moderation has been a condition of the functioning of our system of government. A Conservative

[1] *Op. cit.* p. 122.

once wrote of the Conservative rank-and-file that there has been "a pig-headedness that has sometimes been fatal," and that "if the leaders had waited upon their followers for policy, we should still be eating acorns."[1] It might be said with equal justice of the rank-and-file of the party or parties of the Left that there has been an impatience and lack of practical common-sense that has sometimes been fatal, and that if it had not been for the leadership displayed, the consequences for the community would have been equally disastrous.

The conception of British party leaders as prisoners of party and mere exponents of the spirit of partisanship is not borne out by the historical facts. They have led, or attempted to lead, their parties. They have seldom treated party as an end in itself, and repeatedly they have risen above party. Nearly always they have been a check upon the worst manifestations of partisanship, and responsibility for government, actual or potential, has provided a bond between them.

9. *Changes of Party*

Statesmen have repeatedly co-operated in government with former political opponents when a situation of grave emergency or of political deadlock has overshadowed other considerations, or when former differences have disappeared or become secondary. Quite apart from periods of crisis, we have seen not only individual statesmen and politicians, but whole groups, transfer their support from one of the great composite parties to the other.

[1] K. Feiling, *op. cit.*, p. 175.

A change of party label, though seldom rapid or dramatic, is of common occurrence in this country; it provokes, sometimes, malicious comment, but little serious criticism. It is, of course, no necessary sign of merit to remain in the party into which one is born, or led by early associations, ideas, or interests; nor is it in itself a mark of consistency, since a party itself changes even though it continues to bear the same name. The crudity of the charges of betrayal made on such occasions is easily exposed. The simple-minded denunciator of "treachery" may well be asked what he would have done had he been a Liberal or Radical Unionist in 1886, a Conservative Free Trader in 1846 or 1903, a Labour Pacifist in 1914, or a supporter of Mr. MacDonald in 1931. What is the member of a party to do if his party decides on a course of action, or a particular measure, which he cannot support? Much will depend, of course, upon the gravity of the issues involved. If he regards them as important and urgent, then he is compelled to consider whether or not he can continue in association with his party. It is possible that he may only be able to do so at the price of silent acquiescence. The kind of situation envisaged has been well presented in the following passage:—

"Party is but an instrument for enacting convictions; and a politician's convictions may, like those of Burke, be from the first, or by experience may come to be, far wider than what his chosen party enacts. It does not follow that he need therefore cease to act with it. Of the instruments at his disposal it may remain the best. But a time may come, as it came to Burke, when the divergence between conviction and instrument may become so wide, that the chosen party can be chosen no longer.

A change may pass over the individual's beliefs; they may broaden, or they may undergo an alteration of relative emphasis. Or something may happen in the world of politics, an abuse of power, an industrial crisis, a threatening of turbulence, a war, even perhaps (as in the supreme instance of 1789) a revolution in another country; and, in the light of the new event, political ends may, in their order of urgency, be thrown into a fresh perspective. Or the party itself may change; new counsels may prevail within it, and questions, hitherto slumbering in the background, may be pushed to the front. Happen how it may, the result is the same. The instrument of action, once chosen and cherished, is a fit instrument no longer; even in the teeth of sentiment and of habit, the inevitable hour of rupture comes; and the soldier of party resigns his commission, if indeed he is not forced to take service in the ranks of those he once counted as his life-long foes."[1]

As we have noted, there is no great gulf separating the parties. Even prominent politicians, although their position, perhaps as party leaders, imposes upon them special responsibilities and difficulties, find it relatively easy to change their party allegiance. It is significant also that, having done so, they are able to work as amicably, as a rule, with their new colleagues as with the old. With two great parties only, it is often no easy matter for the politically intelligent individual to decide in which he can work the more effectively. Whichever way he may decide, he is called upon to compromise in practical political activity. With the individual who has become a party leader, the position is even more complex. The leader has to consider not merely his personal position, but the effect of any action he may take upon the fortunes of his party. His influence is

[1] John MacCunn, *Ethics of Citizenship*, p. 91.

greater, and for obvious reasons he is less likely to break with his party. At the same time, his responsibilities are greater than those of the ordinary citizen. He cannot maintain an attitude of aloofness to any important development in the policy of his party: usually, he is compelled to declare his attitude. The difficulty may arise, indeed, because the party refuses to follow a course of action he has proposed. Hence it happens that the party leader, or prominent party man, while normally endeavouring to avoid action likely to split his party, is sometimes compelled to take such action. It is noteworthy that statesmen who have been distinguished and able in their advocacy of party have felt obliged to adopt a course which has involved the severance of their party connections. Burke and Chamberlain are famous instances; and Mr. MacDonald provides a more recent case of the same thing.

Once a leader has broken with the main body of his party, the future of himself and any followers he may have in relation to the parties will depend upon a variety of contingencies. The breach may be healed, or the temporary association with the other party, inevitable in the circumstances, may eventually ripen into a permanent alliance. The latter is as likely or more likely than the former, for the occasion of the breach is bound to be of considerable importance. However, in the latter event, it is misleading to regard what happens as a simple "change of party." Owing to the lapse of time, a study of Mr. Joseph Chamberlain's career may now safely be recommended to party bigots and cynical "intellectuals."

Mr. Francis Holland, dealing with the situation in 1873, wrote that—

"the time was approaching when every member of the House of Commons at issue with his party on some important question was to find himself, if unwilling to retire or to be driven from public life, confronted with the alternatives either of suppressing his convictions on that question or else of changing sides and adopting bodily all the principles of his whilom antagonists."[1]

The passage is, in one respect, very misleading. It is true that a person in such a predicament may have to "change sides": a temporary severance from his party may eventually leave him no alternative. It does not follow, however, that he will have to adopt "bodily all the principles of his whilom antagonists." The suggestion is based upon a defective appreciation of the nature of our political parties. If they were rigid associations based upon certain clearly-defined principles, and imposing doctrinal tests as a condition of membership, the statement would be justified. But that, as we have seen, has not been the position. If it had been, the two-party system could not have continued to operate, and, in so far as tendencies in that direction have developed, the two-party system has been weakened. But one has only to apply the suggestion to the case of Chamberlain and his followers to see how misleading it is. Chamberlain certainly did not adopt "bodily all the principles of his whilom antagonists"; on the contrary, his association and subsequent alliance with the Conservatives wrought very considerable changes in the policy of the Conservative Party. The point is of much significance. Breakaways from one party, followed by mergers with the other, have played a most vital part in the

[1] May's *Constitutional History of England*, Vol. III, pp. 83–4.

evolution of the two great parties. The inclusion of the Canningites, and still more of the Peelites, in the Whig Party, helped to transform it into a Liberal Party. The association with the Irish Party, and the subsequent informal alliance with the new Labour Party, led, in the one case, to a deflection, and, in the other, to a new orientation of Liberal Party policy. So, on the other side, the old Tory Party has been transformed by the succession of influxes into its ranks from the Left. It has been an "ever-repeated process," and has contributed as much as any other single factor to that adaptation of party to changing circumstances and new ideas which is a necessary condition of the maintenance of the two-party system in particular, and of parliamentary government in general.[1] The nature and significance of breaches in party unity, and consequent changes of party allegiance are often misunderstood. Divergence from party policy; secession from the main body of the party; "change of party"; do not necessarily imply any change of opinion. The notion that a group of people transferring their support from one party to another either abandon their previous convictions or adopt those of their new party is hopelessly wide of the mark. The effect of any movement of this kind is to change the balance of opinion in both the parties concerned, and the extent to which the position is affected depends, primarily, upon the magnitude of the movement. In any event, the two parties are no longer what they were before.

[1] Mr. Feiling, addressing Conservatives, has said that "If it were possible to enlarge our phylacteries a little less and our historic consciousness a little more, we should think that Liberalism is Conservatism in the making, and that Toryism is the Liberalism of the past."

10. *Summary of the Position*

British parties, then, as we have known them, are not solid blocks of devoted partisans, but bodies comprising many diverse elements, and the lines of demarcation between them are consequently shadowy. There is a large body of central opinion not wholly committed to one side or the other, and most important issues to some extent cut across the nominal party distinctions. The parties are dependent all the time upon the support of outside elements among the general public, and upon the maintenance of their internal cohesion. Consequently, they have had to be broadly "national" in composition and policy.

The practical exigencies of government necessitate avoidance of the dramatic reversals of policy which might follow from the alternation of parties in power; and the violent oscillations alleged to result from the system do not in fact occur. A British party is virtually compelled to pursue a moderate course; if it does not do so, then it suffers a reverse. Leaders, invariably, have been moderates, if not by choice, then of necessity At the same time, they have had to deal with party followings always comprising considerable elements of opposition to their policies of moderation. They have had to attempt to lead unwilling partisans into the necessary paths of compromise, and, sometimes, as individuals, their efforts have failed. But extremist policies or movements, on one side or the other, have always led to a transference of support on the part of the steadying and balancing elements in the centre.

Understanding of these facts about our party system

would do much to eliminate petty, if bitter, controversies from our political life, and would also clear up a great deal of confusion and counteract much of the consequential scepticism about politics and politicians. If a sound sense of proportion is brought to the study, our political "apostates," from Strafford and Shaftesbury and Halifax and Harley, down to Burke and Peel, Chamberlain, Churchill, and MacDonald, are seen to be men of remarkable consistency in essentials, and men of courage into the bargain. More important still, these facts about our parties illuminate the issues raised in our modern controversies about parliamentary government. Failure to grasp them is the source of much misunderstanding. When and in so far as they are appreciated, the picture they present is often regarded as highly unattractive. They are made the basis of a criticism of the system of government of which they are an integral part. It is suggested that the conditions and practices an outline of which has been here attempted are capable of a convincing defence. Are they not, in fact, the necessary conditions of parliamentary government, and of democracy?

CHAPTER IV

DEMOCRACY

1. *Introduction*

BEFORE proceeding further, we must necessarily make some reference to the general subject of democracy. It would be preferable, perhaps, to confine ourselves strictly to the facts of the British system of government and British political practice. That, however, is inexpedient, for discussions concerning our political institutions are now inextricably interwoven with discussions about democracy. Our system of government is criticised both as being democratic and as being imperfectly democratic. On the one hand, it is regarded as an example of democracy in practice, and general criticisms of democracy are applied indiscriminately to it; while, on the other hand, it is held to be defective from the democratic standpoint, and general arguments in favour of democracy are utilised against it. In some quarters, indeed, it is passionately denied that our political institutions are democratic at all.[1] That they are imperfect from the democratic (or from any other) standpoint will be readily granted, for perfection is not to be expected in political institutions any more than in the men and women who create and work them. Much depends,

[1] See G. D. H. Cole, "Notes on Democracy and Dictatorship," *The Highway* (November, 1933).

of course, upon one's interpretation of the term "democracy," but many of the arguments employed to show the defectiveness of our system from the standpoint of democracy are unacceptable, either from that or from any other standpoint; and, as might be expected, the amendments proposed, and the alternatives favoured, are for the most part anything but democratic.

2. *Direct Opposition to Democracy*

We do not propose to make much more than a passing reference to avowedly anti-democratic criticisms, since most modern variants upon these themes are disguised in the language of democracy itself. Frank opposition to democracy is almost as ancient as the first experiments in democracy. From Plato onwards, there has always been criticism of the ignorance, incapacity and passions of the "mob," or of the majority, and advocacy (in very general terms and a variety of guises) of government by the wise or the good or the expert or the truly-patriotic and public-spirited. The worship of the autocratic ruler as "saviour" is, indeed, as old as the hills, and has been a constantly recurring element in the history of mankind. Unfortunately, great difficulty is experienced, now as always, in producing any conviction that the critics of democracy are, politically, less ignorant, more competent, or less liable to the extravagances of passion than the "mob" or the majority. We still encounter the assumption that there is some peculiar virtue in a minority just because it is a minority, and we still have the same deplorable lack of clarity about which

minority is *the* minority. We are not told how to
distinguish between the pretensions of rival would-be
"saviours"; nor is any guidance given on the rather
important problem of how we are to know and to
select from the wise or the good or the expert or the
truly-patriotic or public-spirited, or whether we are
to leave it to them to arrange or to fight it out for
themselves.

For the most part, anti-democratic criticisms of
the kind referred to are based upon assumptions which
do not fit the political facts in this country. It has been
pointed out already that the dangers and defects to
which they call attention have been largely avoided
here as a consequence of the nature of British political
development. The "democracy" criticised is an
abstract conception bearing little relation to the
actual system of government operating in this country,
or, indeed, to any system of representative government. Neither here nor elsewhere is there strictly
any such thing as "government by the people." Even
Parliament does not govern directly. Crude popular
outbreaks of political passion seldom result in precipitate governmental action; they are canalised into
relatively harmless channels. The criticisms referred
to not only ignore, to a large extent, the conditions
of the *representative* system, but also ignore the particular form which that system has taken in this
country, and the methods by which it is here operated.
They neglect the relations of the executive to the
legislature described in Chapter I, and the scope
available, and in fact utilised, for expert political and
technical guidance. The practical limitations of
"majority rule," to which some reference has already

been made, are also overlooked. Indeed, it may justly be contended that insufficient attention is given by critics of this type to the practical limitations of government itself. All governments are dependent, to greater or less extent, upon the "consent" of the people. (In this respect, the difference between a supposedly "democratic" system of government (i.e. one based upon a wide or universal franchise), and a system based frankly upon the rule of some select minority (or majority), is one of degree only, and not of kind.[1] Modern dictatorships not only rest upon "the consent of the people," but also challengingly proclaim the fact./ Nor can the handicaps arising from popular ignorance and inertia be evaded by rejection of democratic methods. The stupidity, the prejudices and the passions of the ordinary citizen are reflected as much (or more) in the "dictatorships" as in the Parliaments and Cabinets of the "democracies." Indeed, one at least of the post-war dictatorships has been the outcome of what can only be described as mass-hysteria, affecting all classes of the community.

3. *Democracy as a Political Method*

The extent of the confusion prevailing to-day upon the subject of democracy will be realised by anyone who has followed the current controversy about "democracy" and "dictatorship." Both these terms have been so much abused of late that the distinction between them has been largely obscured. That is

[1] "If despotic Government comes into anything like habitual conflict with the unwritten law which represents the general will, its dissolution is beginning."—T. H. Green, *Principles of Political Obligation*, p. 102.

partly because, in spite of the recent tendency to deride democratic institutions, their appeal is still so powerful that the partisans of dictatorship seldom proclaim their aims frankly and directly. "Democracy," in consequence, has suffered rather more than "dictatorship" from misinterpretation. It has become one of our "blessed words," charged with so many meanings that it runs the risk of becoming meaningless for purposes of rational discussion.

The misuse of the term "democracy" is a measure of the homage which dictators pay to democracy, and their efforts in this connection are facilitated by the misuse of the term by others. It is instructive to note the attempts to prove all dictatorships "real democracies," and all democracies "veiled dictatorships." In Soviet Russia, we are often told, there is more "real democracy" than in this country.[1] After

---

[1] The pathetic but sincerely held belief of many people in the democratic nature of the Communist régime is largely due, apart from other elements of confusion, to a failure to appreciate the artificiality of the system of Soviets. Dr. Arthur Rosenberg, who is strongly sympathetic towards Communism, has written on this subject as follows:—"In 1917 Lenin used the Soviets to destroy Tsarism." (In fact, of course, to destroy the Provisional Government.) "Once that had been accomplished he created his own State machinery after the true Bolshevik pattern, i.e. the rule of a small disciplined minority of professional revolutionaries over the great and undisciplined masses. Although from a technical standpoint it would have presented no difficulty, the Bolsheviks nevertheless did not abolish the Soviets and instead retained and used them as the decorative outward symbol of their authority. It was through their symbolic use by the Bolsheviks in 1918 and the succeeding years that the Soviets were first brought into a position irreconcilable with true democracy. There can be no more truly democratic institution than a real and efficiently working Soviet. The Bolshevik Soviets, on the other hand, have been since 1918 no more than symbols of the rule of a small minority over the broad masses of the nation."—"From the summer of 1918 until the present day the Bolshevik Party has been the sole political Party in Russia enjoying a legal existence. This state of affairs has brought about the death of Soviet democracy. In elections for the Soviets the choice of the

all, did not the Bolsheviks attain power by an appeal to democracy?[1] Even Mussolini has declared that "Fascism may write itself down as 'an organised, centralised and authoritative democracy';"[2] and Hitler, also, is prepared to assert, on occasions, that National Socialist Germany is a democracy. Our own would-be dictators, whether on the Right or on the Left, nearly all proclaim themselves enthusiastic democrats, hoping thus to be allowed quietly to have their own way. They desire to act as dictators while retaining the forms of democracy, and to enjoy the advantages of dictatorship without incurring any of its customary pains and penalties.

Democracy is sometimes defined as a particular form of government; and sometimes, not only as such, but also, and primarily, as a kind of social life, a kind of civilization.[3] Some interpretations, indeed, are

---

electors is confined to Bolsheviks or Independents who are pledged to support the Bolshevik Government. Thus all freedom of choice is taken away from the elector and he is the prisoner of the Government. Every Bolshevik member of the Soviet is, moreover, pledged to act in strict accordance with the order of his Party leaders." There is not even a dictatorship of the proletariat. "Although the Bolsheviks have called their rule in Russia since 1918 a dictatorship of the proletariat, it is in reality a dictatorship of the Bolshevik Party or—better said—of the Central Committee of the Party over the proletariat and the entire nation."—*A History of Bolshevism*, pp. 122–3.

[1] "The motto of the Bolshevik Revolution was not 'Dictatorship of the Proletariat! Down with Democracy!' but was its exact contrary, 'Long live Democracy! Down with Dictators!'"—Rosenberg. Ibid. p. 98.

"As a democratic Government we cannot disregard the decision of the masses of the people even if we do not agree with it. If the peasants follow the Socialist-Revolutionaries farther, even if they give that party a majority in the Constituent Assembly, we shall still say: so be it."—Lenin, at the 2nd Soviet Conference, October 26th, 1917.

[2] *The Political and Social Doctrine of Fascism*, p. 16.

[3] A recent discussion between Mr. Leonard Wolff and Lord Eustace Percy may serve as an illustration. Democracy, says Mr.

remarkably comprehensive. There are people who employ the term "democracy" to cover anything and everything they regard as desirable; and there are even some who use it to cover anything they think undesirable.

If the prevalent confusion is to be dispelled, the first and the essential thing to insist upon is that democracy is a *method* of arriving at political decisions. In discussing "democracy" and "dictatorship," for instance, we are discussing alternative ways of taking political action. How else can "democracy" be contrasted with "dictatorship"? It is difficult to interpret dictatorship in any other way than as a particular set of political methods, resulting in a particular type of government. It seems, however, that the same difficulty is not experienced in the case of democracy, and in this connection we venture to assert that discussion of the "democratic ideal," however legitimate and even admirable, has in practice tended both to distract attention from the

---

Wolff, "is really a way of looking at things, a political and social ideal, the ideas that people have of the kind of government they want, the kind of country or society or civilization they want to live in. . . . You cannot define democracy in a single sentence because it . . . tries to answer this question, What kind of government, social life, and civilization do we want? Democracy is, therefore . . . a complicated thing, for it must consist of a number of different ideas about politics and society and the lives that ordinary people ought to live." Mr. Wolff summarises the larger ideas underlying democracy as relating, first, to the everyday happiness of ordinary people, secondly, to equality, and thirdly, to liberty. Lord Eustace Percy's comment was: "I think Mr. Wolff confuses what democracy is with the things that he would like democracies to do. He would like democracy to promote the happiness and freedom of the individual and to give him equality of opportunity, mainly through education. Therefore, he says that these things are democracy. But democracy is a form of government. . . . And I am afraid it is rather difficult to prove that the things that Mr. Wolff wants democracies to do are the things that democracies usually do and that other forms of government usually fail to do."—*The Modern State*, pp. 52–3 and 123.

relevant problems and to muddle the minds of men in dealing with them. Some people, for instance, identify democracy with economic or social equality; but how can one contrast dictatorship with economic equality? After all, the two things may be compatible. Indeed, the one may be a means of attaining the other. That is why we find people who advocate dictatorship as a means to what they call, erroneously, "democracy."

The root of the trouble is that a habit has been developed of thinking and speaking of "democracy" as a certain kind of social life; and the confusion is increased by reason of the fact that people differ a great deal about the kind of social life which they describe as "democratic." On this view, "democracy" becomes something affecting every aspect of the life of men in society. It loses its specifically political connotation. "Democracy" becomes "social," "economic," "industrial," according to the particular aspect of social life in which one is interested. In so far as it is treated as a political phenomenon, it is thought to consist of certain results brought about by political action, certain things which are done, or which ought to be done, by Governments. It is less frequently thought of as a system of government or as a method by which a community decides *what* is to be done. And even when it is thought of in that kind of way, it is labelled "political democracy," and dismissed, often enough, as a matter of secondary importance.

This attitude towards democracy needs to be decisively rejected. The meaning of democracy has been unduly enlarged, and a stricter interpretation must be consistently adhered to if the widespread confusion now existing is to be cleared up. In its

I

original meaning, democracy signified a particular type of government, viz.: one in which the general body of citizens were able to participate in the control and direction of the affairs of the community; and that should provide the starting point for an interpretation of democracy.

Democracy, it is true, is not a mere matter of the *form* of political institutions. On the other hand, it is essentially a matter of political *method*. It is the confusion of ends with methods which is so largely responsible for obscuring the distinction between democracy and dictatorship. Democracy does not consist in getting certain things done, but in a certain *way* of doing things. The things done may be wise or unwise, good or bad; they may be of this kind or of that kind; we may like them or we may dislike them; such points are irrelevant. Democracy is not a particular kind of civilization: it is rather a civilized way of taking political action. Dictatorship, though often hailed nowadays as a new method of salvation, is, in fact, a reversion to the methods of a relative barbarism.

4. *Democracy and Equality*

No doubt, the ideas and ideals from which democracy has sprung are not exhausted by it. They can be, and to some extent have been, applied beyond the sphere of political method to other aspects and problems of social life, and the connection may seem to justify the extension of the meaning of democracy. None the less, the resultant confusion may have regrettable consequences. Current controversy shows that plainly enough. We find "political democracy" contrasted with "true democracy"; "formal democracy" with "real democracy"; "capitalist democracy" with "pure democracy." Of course, such expressions as "pure democracy" or "true democracy" may be used in a restricted sense to indicate merely the ideal or perfected democratic method, but, unfortunately, they are usually given a much wider interpretation, and, in order to secure what is called "real" or "true" or "pure" democracy, i.e. all kinds of things having no necessary connection with the democratic method, some people will actually advocate the methods of violent revolution and dictatorship. So it is, again, with "economic democracy" or "social democracy." To get "economic democracy," i.e. economic equality, people will advocate policies which, in fact, involve the abandonment of democracy as a political method. Thus we have the paradoxical position that democracy is attacked in the name of "democracy," and sometimes sacrificed to the achievement of "democracy."

Professor Hans Kelsen has pointed out[1] that the misuse of the word democracy to indicate, e.g. economic equality or justice, a particular economic system or social order, has enabled the word to be twisted and diverted to the service of political dictatorship. Consciously or unconsciously, the terminology of democracy is being employed to the detriment of democracy. Much trouble would be avoided, for instance, if the advocates of economic equality were to refrain from dressing it up so frequently in the guise of democracy. As Professor Kelsen insists, it has no necessary connection with democracy; the clearest proof of which is that it can be realised, in so far as it is capable of

---

[1] *La Democratie : sa nature—sa valeur*, p. 105.

realisation, under a dictatorial or autocratic régime as well as or better than under a democratic régime. In his view, one of the chief sources of the prevalent confusion is the unwarranted identification of democracy and equality. It is an essential part of his thesis that the basic idea of democracy is not equality, but liberty; the idea of equality enters in, but only as formal equality in liberty, equality of political rights. Historically, the struggle for democracy has been one for political liberty, and it is, of course, the loss of political liberty which provides the feature common to all successful non-democratic movements, those which are egalitarian in motive as much as those which are not.

We are often told that without equality political liberty is a fraud and a delusion. It is, doubtless, incomplete, but its reality and value are appreciated when deprivation of it becomes probable or actual. Recent events in Germany have done much to awaken people to its importance. In this country, we have been taking it too much for granted, and in some quarters exaggeration of its imperfections has resulted in a dangerous disparagement of the actual measure of political freedom we enjoy. It is important, therefore, that the elements in the situation should be set out in their correct proportions.

Democracy, we have urged, is a method of arriving at political decisions, and, that being the case, it is clearly not identifiable either with equality or with liberty. At the same time, we are prepared to maintain that the democratic method springs from and is based upon the conception of freedom. This does not mean, however, that freedom in the full sense is a necessary

condition either of the existence or of the satisfactory
working of democracy. What we are concerned with
is only one particular aspect of social life, viz.: the
taking of political decisions, and the freedom which is
requisite or desirable is freedom in that sphere. Even
so, this political liberty involves a measure of equality.
It implies, as we have noted, equality of political rights;
and it is incomplete in so far as avoidable inequalities
impair the exercise of these rights and thereby diminish
its reality.

Granted, however, that the democratic method might
function more satisfactorily if existing inequalities were
removed or counteracted, it is not true that the
democratic method is nullified by the existence of
any such inequalities. Equality is not a necessary
condition of the *existence* of democracy: it may be a
condition of its *improvement*, but only of its improvement. In view of egalitarian exaggerations, it is well
to remember that that which it is desired to improve
must exist. It may be noted also that the defects
actually arising from inequalities are not by any means
the only defects to be found in the working of the
democratic method. Democracy, for instance, would
function more satisfactorily if all citizens were exclusively actuated by a desire to promote the common
good, but the fact that we have not attained, and
perhaps never shall attain, to that ideal situation does
not mean that it is impossible to proceed by the
democratic method, or that any other method is
preferable.

It is necessary, however, to make some enquiry
into the nature of the equality which is regarded as
indispensable to the fully satisfactory working of the

democratic method. Those who criticize democracy from the egalitarian standpoint invariably interpret equality as "economic equality," or equality of incomes. They argue, in the words of Mr. J. A. Hobson, that "effective political democracy is unattainable without economic equality."[1] Is this emphasis upon economic equality justified? Why should the successful working of the democratic method be dependent upon equality of incomes? The extent and value of the political contribution one is capable of making is neither determined by nor proportionate to the size of one's income. The possession of a greater or lesser income than others enjoy does not necessarily imply an advantage or a handicap. To say that effective political democracy is unattainable without economic equality is certainly no more justifiable than to say that it is unattainable without intellectual equality. The latter is, of course, impossible of attainment, and there are many who contend that economic equality, whether desirable or not, is also impossible. The equality that is desirable from the democratic standpoint is equality of opportunity for every citizen to make the fullest possible contribution to the democratic process that he or she is capable of making. Economic inequalities constitute only one, and not perhaps the most important, factor in the situation.

It will be readily conceded that the elimination or diminution of existing economic inequalities would facilitate the removal of certain defects in the operation of the democratic method. The economic egalitarians, however, are not content with that admission. The arguments they use imply that the democrat cannot

[1] *Democracy and a Changing Civilisation*, p. 111.

consistently oppose economic equality as undesirable, and that, from the democratic standpoint, the controversy about that particular end is closed. This attitude is in part the outcome of an illegitimate identification of equality with equality of incomes. The democrat as such is only concerned with economic inequalities in so far as they do in fact militate against the successful working of democracy. Moreover, as a citizen, he has also to consider whether or not economic equality is desirable on general grounds. That the democratic method would function better under conditions of economic equality is not a sufficient basis for acceptance of economic equality. It would be foolish to advocate the achievement of a particular end, considered undesirable on other grounds, merely because of its incidentally desirable effects upon the functioning of political methods. It would be legitimate, therefore, for the democrat to hold the view that it is better to forego that measure of improvement which the achievement of economic equality might render possible in the working of the democratic method. The desirability or otherwise of economic equality is, in fact, just as much a subject of controversy amongst those who accept democratic methods as it is amongst those who do not. Decisions in regard to this, as in regard to other matters, have to be taken either by the democratic method or by some alternative method, even though all available methods may be imperfect, as in fact they are. The opponents and the advocates of economic equality are alike confronted by a choice of methods, and opponents may decide for the methods of democracy just as advocates of economic equality may decide against them.

Finally, with regard to the contention so frequently advanced by economic egalitarians that their particular end must be achieved before democratic methods can be effectively applied, by what methods do they propose to achieve that end? If, indeed, it is true that complete equality (or complete freedom) is an indispensable condition of democracy, it would follow that it is impossible to secure improvements in democracy by democratic methods. That is surely an untenable position. Even if we assume that the attainment of economic equality is desirable, either for itself or in order to improve the working of democratic institutions, the questions at once arise, How is it to be secured? Are democratic methods to be pursued or not? The prior question of method has thus to be answered, whatever the imperfections of the alternative methods available.

5. *Liberty the Basis of Democracy*

We have already admitted that the idea of equality is inseparably connected with democracy, but historically and fundamentally democracy rests upon the idea of freedom. It is the desire for freedom in the political sphere that has provided the driving force behind the advocacy of democratic methods; and, incidentally, it is the denial or drastic restriction of political freedom which is the common factor in all dictatorships.[1]

[1] "The question is not merely who shall rule nor how wealth shall be distributed, but how men shall treat their fellow-men. Is one man to admit the right of another to his own opinion? Or is one to be master and the other an instrument of his will? That is the real issue between Democracy and Dictatorship, as it has lately been fought out in Germany, and as it stood some few years ago in other

The liberty which it is sought by the methods of democracy to ensure and to realise more fully is not, of course, the mere power to do whatever one has a mind to do; nor is it "measured by the number of restraints we do not have." There is, for instance, no necessary connection, whatever historical association there may have been, between democracy and the laissez-faire "individualism" of the nineteenth century. The identification of democracy with "liberalism" of that type has given rise to the erroneous idea that democracy involves a limitation of the field of positive State action. Democracy, on the contrary, is quite consistent with the widest possible extension of the functions of the State, for what matters is that the social order resulting should be created and maintained in accordance with decisions reached by the democratic method. For the same reason, it follows, of course, that there is no necessary incompatibility between democracy and "individualism" or "economic liberalism."

The idea of freedom upon which democracy is based springs from the recognition of man as a being capable of determining his own life with reference to a good, the value of which is lost in being enforced. Not that man necessarily regards himself as being thus determined; indeed, it is precisely because he does not always thus regard himself that discipline is an indispensable adjunct to freedom. Government performs in the life of the community a function analogous to that performed by parental authority in the life of the family. The child is disciplined for its own good,

countries which have established Dictatorships."—Professor Delisle Burns, *The Spectator*, June 16th, 1933.

and disciplined, not in order to serve a parent's purposes, but with a view to developing its own capacity for freedom. Similarly, government, instead of being incompatible with freedom, provides an indispensable basis for its realization, not only in so far as it "hinders hindrances" to freedom, but also inasmuch as it furnishes opportunities for the citizen to acquire and to develop a sense of moral responsibility. For man is not free but enslaved when he seeks merely the satisfaction of his own unrestrained desires. He becomes free when and in so far as he endeavours to act as a moral being.

Nevertheless, just as the heavy hand or the natural influence of the parent can thwart or warp the moral development of the child, so government may hamper or distort that of the adult citizen. Parental discipline, avowedly imposed upon the child "for its own good," may be exercised, in reality, merely to suit the convenience of parents. Similarly, the laws of the State, purporting to promote the good of the community, may be designed, in fact, to further the selfish purposes of those who wield governmental authority. Governmental encroachments upon individual freedom, indeed, have often been extensive, and sometimes arbitrary, and not less so when governmental authority has been exercised ostensibly on behalf of the good of the community. Even when authority is exercised under the rule of law, restrictions upon individual freedom may, nevertheless, accrue as a result of the disparity between law and developing morality. The system of laws formulated and enforced by the State in accordance with past and passing aims and moral conceptions may, and in fact does, conflict with the developing ideas and purposes of the individual. This disparity indicates the existence of differences of opinion concerning morality and the conditions of its advancement. The individual cannot, without loss of freedom, merely acquiesce in a moral code imposed upon him by some external authority. Hence arises a demand that political decisions should be taken only after discussion and according to rules which give all individuals opportunity for participation in the process. For political freedom, in the words of Professor L. T. Hobhouse, "is just the right of every man bound by decisions to contribute whatever it is in him to contribute to the making and remaking of those decisions."[1]

The problem may be stated in another way. Is it possible so to determine the law that men will have, and will feel that they have, an obligation to respect it? Only so can they obey without consciousness of constraint. They will not feel any such obligation unless the objective sought is a common well-being in which they share. Yet the ends which people believe to be good differ greatly. How are such differences to be reconciled? Nor will men feel any such obligation if they have no part in the determination of what they are called upon to obey; if the law is imposed upon them by some external authority. In such circumstances, they will obey, not from any sense of obligation, but only from fear of the possible consequences of disobedience.[2] The desire for freedom leads in

---

[1] *The Elements of Social Justice*, p. 88.

[2] "How far in any particular act of conformity to law the fear of penalties may be operative, it is impossible to say. What is certain is, that a habit of subjection founded upon such fear could not be the basis of political or free society; for to this it is necessary, not

consequence to a demand for the collective determination of the rules by which the mutual relations of men are to be regulated. On what basis, however, is this collective determination of the law to be conducted? How can it be truly collective? Majority rule, for instance, may leave the minority or minorities no more free than if they were under the rule of an autocrat or an oligarchy. Mere "consent" is not enough, for that may be secured under conditions in which political freedom is drastically curtailed or non-existent, and in which there is little or no real power of choice.

Democratic methods of government were evolved in response to such questions. The task of reconciling the freedom of the individual with the authority of the State has always constituted a major problem of politics, and it will be generally conceded that a theoretical solution of the problem can be provided only on democratic lines. In practice, an approximation to its solution can be effected by the democratic method.

6. *The Meaning of Democracy*

Democracy constitutes an attempt to reconcile freedom with the need for law and its enforcement. It may be defined as a political method by which every

---

indeed that everyone subject to the laws should take part in voting them, still less that he should consent to their application to himself, but that it should represent an idea of common good, which each member of the society can make his own so far as he is rational, i.e. capable of the conception of a common good, however much particular passions may lead him to ignore it and thus necessitate the use of force to prevent him from doing that which, so far as influenced by the conception of a common good, he would willingly abstain from."—T. H. Green, *op. cit.*, p. 126.

citizen has the opportunity of participating through discussion in an attempt to reach voluntary agreement as to what shall be done for the good of the community as a whole. It resolves itself, in practice, into a continuous search for agreement through discussion and compromise, and action on the basis of the maximum measure of agreement obtainable.

Discussion, as full and free and wide as possible, is essential. Democracy involves the pooling of ideas and views; it implies a willingness to persuade, and an openness to persuasion. The facts are recognized that there are differences of opinion concerning political ends, and that all men are fallible. Democracy, therefore, is based upon tolerance, and necessitates compromise.[1]

Mere discussion, it follows, is not by itself sufficient. In the first place, it should be directed towards the ascertainment of what is for the good of the community as a whole. The democrat may have a strong conviction of the soundness of his own view of what is for the common good, but, confronted by conflicting views, often held with equal assurance, he is not prepared to assume the correctness of his own. Secondly, discussion should be motivated by a desire to reach agreement. Without that desire, discussion is futile. "The creativeness of discussion," as Dr. A. D. Lindsay has pointed out, "assumes a common purpose animating those who take part in it." . . . "The moment that those discussing begin to play for their own hands, or try to enforce their own personal will, the purpose of the discussion is lost."[2] And the purpose is to reach

[1] See below, Chapter VI, Section 1, p. 148.
[2] *The Essentials of Democracy*, pp. 45-6.

voluntary agreement about what is to be done for the common good.

Dictatorship, on the other hand, is a political method by which one part of the community imposes its will upon the rest of the community, denying to the rest of the community the opportunity of influencing political decisions. The dictators may be few or numerous, and they may or may not have majority backing. Even where they have such backing, it is largely meaningless and unreal, because it is not the outcome of free discussion, and because there is no real freedom of choice. The penalisation of unpalatable opinions, the consequent restriction and distortion of discussion, the suppression of all oppositionist political associations, are distinguishing marks of dictatorships. Under a dictatorship, there is no enquiry into what is for the common good. The dictator or dictators *know* what is for the good of the community; they assume, that is to say, that they are right; and because they are convinced of the rightness of their opinions, they feel justified in enforcing them upon the rest of the community.[1]

Further consideration of the meaning of democracy will help to make the distinction between the two methods clear. There are, however, certain practical difficulties in the way of the operation of the democratic method. The scale of the modern community compels the selection not only of representatives but also of executive agents. The expression "government by the people" is, therefore, misleading. The practical

---

[1] "The greatness of any active organisation, which is the embodiment of an idea, lies in the spirit of religious fanaticism and intolerance in which it attacks all others, being fanatically convinced that it alone is right."—Adolf Hitler, *My Struggle*, p. 138. General Goering has attributed to Hitler a more than Papal infallibility.

problems involved make it impossible even for the representatives of the people in Parliament assembled themselves directly to conduct the executive government. All citizens, however, can influence political decisions; they can all participate in the discussions which precede those decisions; and they can all exercise a measure of control over their representatives, and, through them, over the executive government. Nevertheless, it follows from the facts of size and numbers that the processes of discussion and control must be conducted by stages.

At no stage, however, is it possible, in practice, to secure anything approaching unanimous agreement, and yet decisions have to be taken. Therefore, the device of voting has to be introduced, with its corollary of acceptance of majority decisions. That, in turn, may involve the provision of safeguards against abuse of power by majorities, as by representatives as such, or by executive agents. And these practical points make it clear that there is bound to be a wide margin within which reliance has to be placed upon conformity to the spirit of the democratic method.

Obviously, no government can function if all its actions have to be approved by every citizen in the community. Unanimity is unattainable. Indeed, in the complex conditions of the modern world, it is more difficult than ever before to secure voluntary agreement even among a majority of the community Yet, without a majority, democratic government cannot function, and without a fairly stable majority it cannot function well.[1]   At the same time, mere "majority

---

[1] It is important to note that the two-party arrangement does ensure a measure of agreement normally sufficient to provide a

rule" would not satisfy the demand for political freedom. There is no more hopeless and crushing form of tyranny than the tyranny of a majority.

The assumption is often made that democracy in practice amounts to nothing more than the rule of the majority, or the rule of those who have the support of a majority, and that a policy or a particular measure conforms to the requirements of the democratic method if it has majority backing.[1]

That is not the case. It is clear that no distinction between democracy and dictatorship can be based upon the presence or absence of "majority rule." The difference between the two methods is not that between a majority imposing its will upon the rest and a minority imposing its will upon the rest. Indeed, modern dictatorships often have, or soon acquire, majority backing. Nowadays, it is part of the technique of the would-be dictator to acquire a majority under the forms of democracy.[2] If democracy means nothing more than "majority rule," then the National Socialist régime in Germany to-day is almost certainly democratic. We suggest that, under democratic conditions, "the right of the majority to act upon its purposes" is not unconditional. The minority has limiting rights; the right to influence the conduct of public affairs by the free expression of its opinions

---

fairly stable majority backing for a comprehensive political policy Under multi-party conditions, the need for securing agreement remains, but it is more difficult to get, and when secured it is, as a rule, less satisfactory and less stable in its nature.

[1] "All who believe in democracy must also believe in majority rule. That is the essence of democracy."—The Right Hon. G. Lansbury, *The Clarion*, April 21st, 1934.

[2] It may be noted that British Fascism, according to Sir Oswald Mosley, stands for "government of the people by the majority of the people."

and by free political association; and the right to have its wishes and interests taken into consideration. The majority has an obligation to respect those rights, and to exercise its powers with the utmost restraint and moderation possible in the circumstances. That is the corollary of the minority's obligation to acquiesce in the actions taken by majority decisions.

It has to be remembered also that, under democratic conditions, both majority and minority are the outcome of free discussion. In default of the unanimous agreement which is ideally desirable, a minority "consents" because it has participated fully and freely in the discussions which have preceded the decisions taken, and in the course of which both majority and minority have emerged. The "consent" thus forthcoming differs in its nature from the plebiscitary "consent" sometimes accorded to dictatorships. That which distinguishes democracy from dictatorship in this respect is not the *number* of citizens "consenting," but the conditions under which the "consent" is elicited. The vital point, once again, is the presence or absence of freedom, not only in the process of voting, but also, and much more important, in the preceding process of discussion. It follows that it is most inadequate to regard democracy as "government by consent of the governed." "Consent" by itself is not sufficient, although it may be all that is forthcoming from particular individuals. Moreover, "consent" may be secured by other political methods, and in an interesting variety of ways. If "consent" were the sole criterion, the Hitler régime in Germany, like Italian Fascism, would be almost perfectly "democratic." After all, what more remarkable

K

expression of "consent" has ever been given than the Fascist vote at the Italian Parliamentary Election of March, 1934?

Democracy, on the view presented, is not just a matter of counting heads instead of breaking them, although that is not the least of the virtues which may be claimed on its behalf. Of course, it is not claimed that the opportunities provided by the democratic method are equal for all citizens: it is probably impossible to secure that. The existence of opportunities does not imply that they are fully utilised. In practice, many people shirk their democratic responsibilities. Nor is it suggested that the contributions made are of equal value. Moreover, no one would contend that all citizens are, in fact, animated by a desire to reach agreement, or by concern for the well-being of the community as a whole. The respects in which practice falls short of the ideal indicate the main defects in any particular democratic régime, and the more important directions in which improvement may be made.

7. *Democracy and British Parliamentary Government*

The question arises, Is British Parliamentary government democratic? That it is imperfect from the democratic standpoint is true enough, but its imperfections do not warrant denial of its title to be regarded as democratic. Dictatorships, past and present, have been none the less dictatorships because they have been or are defective when judged from the standpoint of the ideal dictatorship (if, indeed, there is any such thing). The contention that we are not in enjoyment of democracy derives what little plausibility it has from the illegitimate identification of democracy with economic or social equality. Our political institutions and practices are founded essentially, if not completely, upon the democratic method. Indeed, without the key provided by that method it is impossible fully to understand the phenomena of British political life discussed in the preceding chapters. The democratic nature of British parliamentary government is confirmed by current criticisms, for most, and the more important, of such criticisms are derived from objection to, or impatience with, the limitations imposed by the need for securing voluntary general agreement.

It is true that with us the democratic method is followed largely from habit. When there is conscious acceptance of it, that acceptance is often reluctant. Moreover, the superficialities of the party struggle obscure the nature of the democratic process. A party apparently endeavours to defeat its rival or rivals, not to convince them. The ordinary member of the Conservative Party is not conscious of any desire to reach agreement with his Liberal or Labour opponents, nor they with him. Indeed, most party men would normally repudiate indignantly the mere suggestion of any such agreement. But, as we have seen, the realities of British political life do not conform to the simple impressions of the average partisan or the casual observer. A party in itself represents a wide measure of agreement, into which compromise enters. It has to concede and persuade in order to acquire majority backing, and even then it cannot with safety impose its decisions dictatorially upon the rest of the community. A victory at a General Election is only a preparatory stage in the taking of decisions. Where there are two great parties only, and the defeated party is almost certain to take office in the course of a few years, the successful party cannot hope to impose its will arbitrarily upon the other. The Opposition is much too powerful, actually or potentially, for such methods to succeed. It exercises considerable influence upon the legislation passed, and upon the general conduct of affairs. Discussion, in Parliament and elsewhere, has its effect. The view, often expressed, that parliamentary discussions are unreal because voting is usually on strict party lines is very superficial. As Dr. Lindsay has reminded us, "Men with inside experience of politics will usually tell you that the effect of an able and critical opposition is seen least in the division lists."[1] The Governmental majority may often be called "cast-iron"; it may be "brutally" or "ruthlessly" used (although such expressions are very seldom justifiable); but what matters is the nature of the policy and proposals the Governmental majority is employed to support and carry. These are always modified in greater or less degree as a result of discussion and criticism.

Of course, majority decisions, even when framed to minimize opposition, remain majority decisions. They have to be taken, but the agreement that cannot be secured in advance is roughly attained in practice by the alternation of the parties in power.[2] That

[1] p. 39, *op. cit.*
[2] "In the alternation in power of political parties there is often worked out in practical dialectic what discussion could not discover."—Dr. A. D. Lindsay, p. 47, *op. cit.*

alternation, as has been noted, imposes a restriction upon reversals of policy, and a continuity which, in fact, represents the agreement reached by the democratic method. So far from the minority being powerless, it is an essential part of the British system of government. As such, it has a status happily indicated by the phrase "His Majesty's Opposition." The desirability of a strong Opposition is a commonplace in commentary upon public affairs in this country. The existence of such an Opposition makes possible a peaceful change of government and re-orientation of public policy. The possibility of providing an alternative administration imposes upon the Opposition a degree of responsibility which might otherwise be lacking. It introduces an element of practicality into political controversy which goes far to bridge differences and to facilitate agreements. The Opposition is not merely tolerated, but treated as indispensable. Here we have another illustration of the vital difference between democracy and its alternative. The democratic method is not that of securing formal agreement by enforcing acceptance of minority or majority decrees through the suppression of all opposition. On the contrary, differences are recognized, and their adequate expression welcomed as a means of attaining voluntary and genuine accord.

Herr Friedrich Sieburg, an apologist of the "Nazi" Revolution, has written of democracy that it "assigns a supreme value to toleration." "Parliamentarism," he says, " properly understood, affords a pattern example of the way in which men can arrive at agreement despite their conflicting interests. Conflict is, in fact, the very essence of the parliamentary system.

The Opposition is no less important than the ruling party, and this legitimisation of the opposition infuses an element of humanity into parliamentary government."[1] Coming from such a quarter, the tribute is valuable, and it confirms the argument of this chapter.

[1] *Germany : My Country*, pp. 121–2.

CHAPTER V

1. *Agreement upon " Fundamentals "*

WHETHER or not the interpretation of democracy given
in the preceding chapter is accepted, and whether
or not our political methods are considered democratic,
it is conceded, as a rule, that British parliamentary
government depends upon a continuous search for,
and achievement of, general agreement. It is asserted,
moreover, that this process is itself conditional upon
the existence of some underlying basis of common
agreement. Current doubts about the future spring
from the view that this common agreement is in course
of dissolution. Some people merely regard its breakdown as contingent upon the emergence of conditions
which may possibly arise in the near future; others
consider that the dissolution is proceeding rapidly;
and yet others maintain that the agreement is already
shattered. The view is that the circumstances, which
enabled the political system to function in the past,
have changed. A situation now exists in which the
requisite basis of agreement may disappear, is in
course of disappearance, or has already disappeared.
Before examining this view in its various aspects,
it is desirable to consider the form in which the main
issue is raised. The argument is that unless there is a
general agreement upon fundamentals there can be

little hope of securing the atmosphere of tolerance and the measure of detailed agreement and continuity requisite for the functioning of parliamentary government. The following quotations illustrate the point (my italics):

"It is essential," writes Mr. G. D. H. Cole, "to the working of the party system," under parliamentary institutions, "that the two rival parties which dominate the situation—however much they may disagree about secondary questions—should be in *close agreement on fundamentals*. Thus in the nineteenth century the Conservative and Liberal Parties in Great Britain differed on a wide range of matters which did not affect *the fundamental structure of society*, but were in essential agreement in wishing to preserve *both Capitalism and the parliamentary institutions which went with it*. . . . A party system of this kind becomes unworkable and inappropriate as soon as there arises a party which, so far from accepting *the fundamentals of the existing order*, desires a complete change of social system, or at any rate as soon as such a party becomes strong enough to occupy a position of primary importance in the political life of the country. . . . When therefore *a fundamental difference of opinion about the right basis of social organisation* comes to dominate political life, the old party system breaks down; and it is natural that each of the rival forces should desire to establish itself permanently and securely in power, and to remove as far as possible all prospect of a return of its rival to office."[1]

Professor H. J. Laski, in his *Democracy in Crisis*, asserts that:

"the doctrines in battle together are mutual and exclusive opposites between which there is no prospect of final

[1] *The Intelligent Man's Guide through World Chaos*, p. 603.

adjustment. A society can no more make peace between the motives of private profit and public service than it can continue half-slave and half-free. There is absent from its *foundations* that area of *common agreement about fundamentals* which makes possible the unity needful for peace."[1]

"So long as the parties to the political equation do not differ seriously about its terms, the device of alternating government and opposition does not matter very seriously since the ultimate unity presupposes the necessary continuity of policy on all matters of essential concern. A party which has been in opposition can, when it comes again into office, take up the threads of its activity more or less where it left them on the previous occasion. It does not need to engage in drastic reconstruction of the measures passed by its predecessor because these will have left unchanged *the fundamental contours of the State*. It can be prepared to accept the risks of the next election because it knows that, in due process of time, it is certain of office again. It is impossible to over-estimate the degree to which the success of parliamentary government is built upon these simple inferences from its basic principle. But we are bound to ask ourselves whether these inferences are justified when the common ground between parties is narrowed so as to exclude that area upon which *the whole character of the system* has previously depended."[2]

Again, in *The Labour Party and the Constitution :*

"Our system has immense successes to its credit. But their root has always been the simple fact that the parties which alternatively governed the country were agreed about *its fundamental way of life*. But the day has passed when political parties were united about the national way of life; they differ to-day, not over the incidentals, but *the foundations of political principle*."[3]

[1] p. 164.   [2] pp. 82–3.   [3] p. 27.

Professor Laski quotes a passage from Lord Balfour's preface to his edition of Bagehot's *English Constitution*, in which that statesman wrote:

"Let the political parties be reduced to two (admittedly the most convenient number for Cabinet Government), but let the chasm dividing them be so profound that a change of Administration would in fact be a revolution disguised under a constitutional procedure. . . . Is there any ground for expecting that our Cabinet system, admirably fitted to adjust political action to the ordinary oscillations of public opinion, could deal with these violent situations? . . . Our alternating Cabinets, though belonging to different parties, have never differed about *the foundations of society*."

The constant refrain is that there must be agreement upon fundamentals; but what are these "fundamentals?" The English politician has a well-grounded distaste for the term. "Weighty as the word appeareth," wrote Halifax, "no Feather hath been more blown about in the World than this word, Fundamental." Nevertheless, Halifax himself was able to lay down some fundamentals, and we may safely grant the existence of certain fundamentals of British parliamentary government. It is important, however, to distinguish between the matters for which a "fundamental" character may be claimed, and to ascertain which really are fundamental in this connection.

A distinction, we suggest, must be drawn between the methods of democracy, or (if it is preferred) the methods hitherto employed in British politics, and the existing economic and social structure. It is the former only upon which general agreement is requisite. If there are any fundamentals in politics, they are the principles of the democratic method. Those accepted, differences about "the right basis of social organisation," about "ways of life," about "the foundations of society," cease to be a danger to parliamentary government. Indeed, differences of that kind are presupposed. They may lead people to reject democratic methods; that is always possible; but it does not necessarily follow. Questions relative to "the economic system" or "the social order" may be thought fundamental, of course. After all, many matters have been so regarded in the course of history, among them religious dogmas and forms of worship. Some of them may possibly have been "fundamental" in one sense or another, but it is quite clear that agreement upon them is not necessary or "fundamental" to parliamentary government. The agreement that *is* requisite is common agreement to seek agreement, and that may not be forthcoming even when differences are "incidental" or "secondary."

The quotations given illustrate the importance of the point. Those who talk of agreement upon fundamentals in this connection are clearly thinking, not of the principles of democracy, but of acceptance or non-acceptance of the existing economic and social order. Mr. Cole has in mind—and to him, apparently, it is the same thing—acceptance of "capitalism" or of "socialism." The same is the case with Professor Laski. True, he writes that, in former times, "the two main parties in Parliament were agreed about the fundamentals of political action," but he interprets this as agreement upon "the kind of state they wanted," and, more definitely, as "substantial agreement upon the vital importance of liberal individualism, especially in the industrial realm."

2. *The Primary Political Question*

The attitude exemplified above provides another instance of failure to distinguish questions of political method from general social arrangements and results. The primary political question is not "*What* are we to achieve?" but "*How* are we to achieve anything we may wish to achieve?" That is the issue which has to be decided. Writers like Mr. Cole and Professor Laski do much to deprive it of its proper significance by refusing to consider it save in relation to their own particular ends. They make the answer to it entirely dependent upon the extent to which political aims diverge, and this, in turn, dependent essentially upon the economic conditions. Their view of parties is much the same as that presented by Mr. Rowse and other Marxists. "The disposition of parties," says Professor Laski, "only reflects the economic conditions of which they are the expression."

But, whatever may be the differences of opinion and interest in the community, the question remains, Are they to be resolved on democratic lines or not? Professor Laski has stated that in the General Election of 1931, "for the first time in British history since the Puritan Rebellion parties confronted one another with respective ways of life which looked to wholly antithetic ends."[1] Assuming that to be true (which it is not), there is still a choice between the methods

[1] *Democracy in Crisis*, p. 39.

of democracy and those of dictatorship and violence. The parallel suggested is instructive, for the Puritan Rebellion taught lessons about non-democratic political methods which have had their effect upon the subsequent course of British history, and which, in the circumstances assumed, may well be recalled. If there is a demand for what are called "fundamental" changes, how is it going to be decided whether or not there are to be changes; what, if any, they shall be; and how they are to be effected? Even on the assumption that "there is in fact only one cleavage"; that society is divided into two great classes with wholly antagonistic interests and aims; that "this contingent clash of mighty opposites" is a reality (which it is not); what is to be done about it? The question of procedure still remains, and parliamentary democracy alone offers any possibility of resolving this conflict of classes without resort to bloodshed.

Many deny the possibility of peaceful agreement in the circumstances envisaged. They use arguments strictly analogous to those employed by the militarists and sceptics in regard to international relations, and with far less justification. We have the same old variations upon the "human nature" theme. Man, it is said, is not fundamentally a reasoning animal. "Reason is powerless to prevent the use of violence when interests conflict to which men attach ultimate importance," writes Professor Laski. "Men only accept the results of reason when these do not deny some end they are determined to obtain."[1] Such statements come strangely from those who preach

[1] *Democracy in Crisis*, p. 159.

determination to obtain a particular end regardless of rational objections either to the end itself or to the particular means proposed. They question the very possibility of compromise, and at the same time significantly denounce compromise as immoral.[1] It is curious that it should be necessary to denounce the impossible so vehemently. It may be "natural" that each of the rival forces postulated should desire "to establish itself permanently and securely in power, and to remove as far as possible all prospect of a return of its rival to power," but it is not inevitable that they should make the attempt. And why should these "intellectual" guides of "fundamentally irrational man" consume so much energy in urging one of the rival forces to take the plunge? Why, indeed, should it be necessary for them to do so? Why not just rely upon "human nature?"

The view presented almost amounts to an assertion that most people (as distinct from Professor Laski) are incapable of exercising reason in their choice of methods, or any ordinary common-sense in the process of attaining their ends; and that they are merely determined to have their own way in all matters which they may happen to regard as "fundamental." That is a view which the democrat must necessarily reject. If it were sound, then parliamentary government would assuredly be doomed.

[1] "If the government is a coalition of parties, the necessity of sinking differences in order to attain the appearance of unity breeds a dishonesty of temper, an accommodation in principle, which saps the moral character of the parliamentary system. There can have been few governments more void of any real moral foundation than the coalitions of 1918 and 1931 in England."—H. J. Laski, *Democracy in Crisis*, p. 78.

3. *Possible Causes of Breakdown*

It may still be true that the requisite common agreement upon which democratic parliamentary government depends is threatened, weakened, or even non-existent. Unless people generally are willing to seek the widest measure of agreement about what is to be done; unless they are prepared to discuss with a view to reaching agreement; unless they are willing to modify their own particular views about what ought to be done; and unless they resist the temptation to impose their own views upon the rest of the community; no kind of democratic government can function satisfactorily. If there are people who are not prepared to tolerate any important change in the existing social order, or if, on the other hand, there are people who are not prepared to accept anything short of an immediate and complete change in the whole social system, then, clearly enough, there is a threat to parliamentary government. If either the one group or the other becomes powerful, then any democratic system of government may be brought to a state of deadlock. Should one of the great British parties take up either attitude, a breakdown of parliamentary government is bound, sooner or later, to ensue. Even in so far as there are only tendencies of this kind, parliamentary government is necessarily weakened.

It should be noted that these results do not follow from the mere appearance of a party which "desires a complete change of social system." They would follow only from a determination to carry out such a change regardless of any objections there may be, or, on the other side, from a similar determination to resist any important change.

4. *The Position in Regard to Methods*

What, however, is the actual situation in this country? That there are elements of danger is fully admitted; they have provided the stimulus for this book, and will receive attention. One of the two great political parties, it is true, has made declarations to the effect that nothing short of a complete and rapid change in the social structure will suffice. It has not yet, however, adopted an avowedly anti-democratic standpoint; on the contrary, it regards itself as the great bulwark of democracy. It has not declared against the parliamentary system, and its repudiation of revolutionary methods is emphatic. No doubt, there is much confusion and inconsistency in its attitude, and this aspect of the matter will be discussed later on, but even those of its members who are clamorous for a "revolutionary policy" display a keen anxiety to pursue it by "constitutional methods." This is as true of the minority who appreciate the difficulties and the dangers to parliamentary institutions involved as of the majority who do not. Indeed, their claim is essentially that they are entitled to equal facilities for applying whatever policy they may propose as are enjoyed by any other party under the existing system of government. When they advocate methods which go beyond normal practices, they often base their case upon real or alleged defects in the existing parliamentary system or upon real or alleged precedents.

As things stand at present, the conclusion is warranted that the important British parties do not differ consciously on questions of political method. There is, of course, the Communist Party, without a single representative in the House of Commons in spite of the economic depression; and there is also the British Union of Fascists, which has not sought representation yet, and the future of which is extremely dubious. At the moment, those who refuse to accept anything less than immediate revolutionary changes, and those who refuse to acquiesce in any measures which, in their opinion, threaten "the foundations of society," constitute relatively insignificant sections of the community, and have shown, as yet, little tendency to grow in numbers. This position may not last, but if it does not do so, that will not be because of the existence or development of differences which are incapable of reconciliation, but owing to avoidable changes in political temper. No differences are unadjustable. Doctrines may be "mutual and exclusive opposites," and, if so, and they remain unchanged, there will be "no prospect of final adjustment" between them. But final adjustments in respect of ultimate ends are not necessary. Politics is a continuous compromise, so that the prospect remains of provisional and partial adjustments, which may provide a basis for modification of the "doctrines" permitting of their "final adjustment." The reconciliation, impossible on the doctrinal plane, may be effected on that of practical politics.

L

5. *The Position in Regard to Aims*

It may well be questioned, further, whether the doctrines referred to have, in fact, that mutually exclusive character which they are so frequently assumed to have. Are "capitalism" and "socialism," in fact, "mutual and exclusive opposites?" Is there no ground common to them, and to their respective supporters?

Both "capitalism" and "socialism" are themselves means to certain ends, and there is no ground for the assumption that the ends must differ. The advocates of both may be, and often are, desirous of achieving the same results. On the other hand, there may be similar differences of aim in each group. Not all Socialists, for example, are in favour of "equality of incomes," and none would claim, of course, that their ideal was more than approximately realisable. "Capitalism" and "socialism" may be defined, of course, merely in terms of the differences between them, but the variety of meanings given to both terms shows that there is not that complete incompatibility so often assumed. "Socialism" may vary from State ownership of the more important branches of production to something different in all respects from "capitalism," no matter how the latter may be interpreted. In between, there are numerous "socialisms," all of which contain important ingredients commonly identified or associated with "capitalism," not to mention that no change is implied in the technique of production or in the technique of the monetary system. Between the "unplanned" economy and the "planned Socialist economy" there is an almost infinite series of possible situations, one of which is, indeed, "the existing situation," and the "planned Socialist economy" itself, of which no clear exposition is as yet available, may take any one of a number of possible forms.[1]

The versions of socialism most favoured in this country to-day would retain or endeavour to retain freedom of choice for consumers and freedom of employment for workers, the general principles of the pricing system, and, necessarily, the phenomena of rent, interest, profits and wages. It is doubtful whether individual interest-receiving, and even individual profit-making, would be entirely eliminated. Private property would not be abolished; it would be recognised, according to one version, "in goods used for personal consumption, but not in goods used for trade or for producing goods to be sold in the way of trade"[2]— a fairly wide field. It is most unlikely that the entire organization of production would be conducted on the collective basis. However, even assuming that socialism involves as its main features the entire abolition of private enterprise and private profit-making, and of inheritance, it is clear that it involves only modifications—important, far-reaching, and difficult to accomplish, no doubt—but still only modifications of "the capitalist system." The changes involved may justly be held to amount to a revolution, but, even so, they do not cover the whole field. Moreover, no economic or social order is "pure"; the "capitalist system" contains alien elements, and so would a "socialist system." The very common identification

[1] See Mrs. Barbara Wootton's *Plan or No Plan*.
[2] H. D. Dickinson, *The Economic Journal*, June, 1933.

of capitalism with "the existing situation" is, of course, quite untenable.

The supporter of capitalism and the advocate of socialism do not confront one another with respective ways of life which are wholly antithetic, or which "look to wholly antithetic ends." The former may not desire economic equality, and the latter may; but the socialist does not desire merely economic equality (very often he does not desire it at all), and the supporter of capitalism may desire much that the socialist desires.

Professor Laski affirms that there can be no peace between the motives of private profit and public service which he obviously considers to be the guiding motives respectively of capitalism and socialism, but this incompatibility does not exist. It is an elementary observation about the economic world that private profit can seldom be made without some production of something the public wants, and it is an elementary deduction from human activity that public service is seldom rendered without some expectation of private reward. The pursuit of private profit can be combined with public service, and, on the other hand, the Socialist may be animated very little by the motive of public service.[1] It

[1] "The economist has little difficulty in showing that the capitalist who is after maximum profit is the servant of the same law as the worker who is after maximum wages; and that the rule that production is not carried on unless it is profitable (if you are careful about the definition of profit, as the economist naturally takes care to be) is not essentially different from the rule that in no well-ordered economic system should we toil at making things that are not worth the trouble of making. Worker, employer, rentier, speculator, all of us get our incomes as the price of something that we do or permit others to do, and the doing, or permitting of which to be done, is an integral part of the business of production; and the attitude of each of us to our own particular price is much of a muchness."—Mrs. B. Wootton, p. 45, op. cit.

should also be recognised by the most ardent Socialist that it is not impossible to defend capitalism on high moral as well as economic grounds. There is not that simple division of motives between Socialists and anti-Socialists which the righteous on both sides so frequently postulate.

6. *The Party Alignment*

We must return from the doctrines of socialism and those of the supporters of capitalism to the actual political situation. Even on the assumption that the differences between those doctrines are "fundamental," they do not provide the basis of party division. Professor Laski's description of the position at the General Election of 1931, quoted above,[1] is rather fantastic. It is scarcely conceivable that he should think of the Labour voters or even of the Labour Party members, as a body of convinced Socialists. Many of the latter were Trade Unionists with little or no love for economic equality, either in theory or practice, or for any socialist scheme. A considerable proportion of the former were Liberal Free Traders; and a goodly number of both sets of people were concerned primarily about immediate and limited matters affecting the social services and wages. The theoretical implications of the issues raised related to political methods, and not to the capitalism-socialism controversy. Socialists were divided about them, and they played the leading parts on both sides. Professor Laski, of course, would deny that those who disagreed with him on that occasion could possibly be Socialists.

[1] See p. 128.

To him, they were people "who accept the foundations of capitalist democracy." That, apparently, is not their view. In his opinion, the division related to "capitalism"; they might well retort that the issue was "democracy."

Even taking the pre-crisis party alignment, it would be very wide of the mark to regard the Labour Party as a Socialist Party or the other parties as composed of supporters of capitalism. The nature of British parties rules out any such clear-cut division. Moreover, the complex lines of division at any particular time are determined by practical issues of limited scope. The real basis of parties is seldom doctrinal, and certainly no British Party has yet been of that type. The Labour Party, in this respect, differs not at all from the other parties. Nor would the position necessarily be altered if it were to call itself a "Socialist" Party. The issues raised by socialist ideas form only part of the subject-matter of politics, and the position in regard to them has certain main outlines which are, in their nature, permanent. Some people approve of the existing social order, apart from minor details; others wish to see it changed. None desire a complete change. Some wish to see some parts altered; others wish to see other parts altered; some desire changes of a certain character; others desire changes of a different character. This kind of situation has always existed, and it is desirable to maintain a balanced historical perspective. People are naturally prone to emphasise points of disagreement, and to attach far greater significance to the problems they have to face and to the issues in which they are interested than the circumstances warrant. Many members

of the Labour Party, for instance, have tended
to look upon their party as entirely different in
kind from other parties, and some of them have never
recovered from the shock of realising that it was
behaving just like any other British party. Many of
their opponents have shared both the estimate and the
surprise. Similarly, each successive economic crisis
has been regarded as the death-knell of "capitalism."
So, also, socialism (to foes as well as friends) is something that strikes at the very foundations of society.
Its importance would not be denied by the assertion
that there is nothing peculiarly "fundamental" in
the socialist controversy. Far-reaching proposals
and movements have existed before socialism, and
whatever exceptional difficulties there may be
relate not so much to the nature of the ultimate
socialist objectives as to the practical problems of
government arising from the extension of State
action involved.

7. *The Dangers to Parliamentary Government*

Our view is that British political parties do not, as
yet, differ "fundamentally" either in regard to social
ideals or political methods. At the same time, democratic methods have never been more than partially
accepted, and practice has always failed to conform
satisfactorily to them. Verbal, and usually quite
sincere, approval of democracy has been accompanied
by refusal or reluctance to accept its implications.
These facts have always constituted a potential danger
to parliamentary government, and in recent years
the danger has become more serious. The root of the

trouble is a failure to appreciate what is involved in the democratic method. That method imposes a restraint which is irritating to most people at times, and to some people all the time. The desire to have one's own way, by force if necessary, is repressed only to rise again. Impatience with the slowness of change displayed on the Left is paralleled on the Right by resentment at demands for further change. On one side, there is a temptation to sweep away the obstructions. Unable to secure by persuasion the necessary basis of consent, people are attracted by the notion of dispensing with or extorting it. On the other side, there is a temptation to put an end to a process of concession which seems to lead only to further concessions. And on each side there is a readiness to attribute the responsibility for a possible resort to force to the obstinacy or perverseness of the other. The attitude adopted is that if force is to be avoided, then the others must give way. This temper is, of course, incompatible with the retention of parliamentary government. It means, on the one side, that people are tempted to run the risk of abandoning parliamentary government in order to defend what they conceive to be their interests, or what they regard as right and proper for the community as a whole. On the other hand, it means that people are so set upon their own particular objective, whatever it may be, and however vague it may be, that they are tempted to subordinate every other consideration to its attainment.

Obsession with particular ends constitutes a special danger. Whether the ends are good or bad, whether the measures designed to achieve them are sound or unsound, the habit of assigning to them an importance that overshadows all other considerations is inconsistent with democratic methods of government. Even if it stops short of an appeal to force, it seriously cripples the working of parliamentary institutions. The objective may be State ownership and control of production, equality of incomes, Free Trade, or the defence of private enterprise; it may be "efficiency," or what is euphemistically called "business government"; it may be anything one likes; the effect, in this respect, is much the same.[1]

8. *The Demand for Action*

More dangerous, perhaps, in present circumstances, than either the impatience of the extreme Left or the obstinacy of the extreme Right, is the demand for action as such[2] All too little attention is given to the inherent difficulties or to the real nature of the problems confronted. Something must be done, dramatically, and done on the large scale. People clamour for "action," for "speed," for "efficiency,"

[1] "The moment a man . . . sets this or that object as an end itself, irrespective of the men who are to reach it, he is bound to become impatient of average stupidity, contemptuous of all rules, legal, moral or customary, which delay the accomplishment of his ends. The desire for some particular reform tends to remove that care for the gradual education of character, which is more important than any given measures, is always so easy to ignore or thrust aside in the enthusiasm of a great cause, and is yet at the basis of all true liberty, whether religious or civil."—J. N. Figgis, *From Gerson to Grotius*, p. 73.

[2] "We are told that Lenin, Mussolini, Mustapha Kemal, and their kind can accomplish what is beyond the power of a free parliament and a slow-moving constitutional executive, that they can override vested interests and obstructive bureaucracies, in a word, that they can deliver the goods. What sort of goods, and at what sort of price?"—Dr. G. P. Gooch, *The Spectator*, March 31st, 1933.

for "leadership," oftentimes scarcely troubling to enquire for what purposes or to what ends. Such questions are dismissed as obstructive, or treated as secondary.

It is doubtless desirable that decisions should be taken without undue delay, and that whatever decisions are arrived at should be translated into action as speedily as possible. The demand for rapid action would have a legitimate basis if it arose merely from avoidable slowness either in the process of reaching decisions or in their application, but that is not in fact the case. It springs partly from impatience, and partly from a craving for mere rapidity and multiplication of movement. To desire speed for its own sake is irrational, and, in politics, as in other spheres of human activity, the indulgence of such a desire may have regrettable consequences. It may well be contended that the world is suffering to-day more from hasty and ill-considered measures than from any dilatoriness in action.

For the most part, however, the demand for action means little more than that action should be taken on the lines favoured by those who present the demand. To them, "inaction" simply means that the actions *they* want taken have not been taken; it does not mean that no actions have been taken. The "speed" they clamour for is speed only in the directions in which *they* want to proceed, although others may not think it wise to tread those particular paths at all. The cry for "leadership" is made usually by those who reject the lead given by others and who demand that others should follow *their* lead, except, indeed, when it arises from a mere abdication of responsibility and takes the form of an impatient longing for a "saviour."

There are some ardent democrats who are so impressed by this attitude that they are over-anxious to identify themselves with it, and are inclined to criticise as negative and unconstructive those who decline to make common cause with them in the matter.[1] If they favour any of the particular actions proposed, or if they are willing to make concessions in the democratic spirit to any such proposals, well and good; but too frequently the standpoint adopted

[1] Lord Allen of Hurtwood, in his able and persuasive book, *Britain's Political Future*, appears to us to fall into this error. His contention that speed is essential in modern politics is based largely upon the view that the impulse in favour of speed is one "which will brook no denial." He admits that this impulse may have dangerous and even disastrous consequences, and that eventually people may be persuaded that it is mistaken, but he contends that for the time being nothing will persuade people to exercise restraint. What, then, becomes of the instrument of reason, for the use of which, here and now, Lord Allen makes so eloquent and powerful an appeal? He seems to argue that, because the reactionary demagogue exploits this emotion in favour of speed for the purpose of acquiring dictatorial power, the democrat must pander to it or "pack up and go out of business."

Lord Allen, it must be noted, writes avowedly from the standpoint of a progressive politician, anxious to attain certain specified objectives. Judged from that standpoint, his book is, in our view, extremely valuable. From the standpoint of political method, however, it is likely to be misleading in certain respects. The methods of democracy are not reserved for the use of progressive politicians only, and it is somewhat unfortunate that Lord Allen should have dealt with them as though they were.

In reality, he advocates speed only in relation to the attainment of his own objectives. Although he introduces and emphasises the contention that speed as such is essential, speedy action in any other direction would not appeal to him. Fortunately for his argument, the impulse in favour of speed, of which he writes, is also, in his view, one that favours speed in the general direction in which he himself wishes to proceed.

The position is similar in regard to his discussion of Leadership. In advocating a new technique of Leadership in "progressive politics," Lord Allen conveys the impression that there can be no Leadership worthy of the name which is not Leadership in the direction in which he wishes this country to move.

is: "If these people are not allowed to have their own way, they will abandon democratic methods; therefore, in order to save democracy, we must second their demands." That, we suggest, involves concessions to a spirit which is alien to parliamentary democracy, and, so far from helping to save it, only weakens it still further.

We grant that if there is a widespread demand for "action," the statesman is obliged to take the fact into consideration. His course has always to be determined in relation to the actual circumstances. He has to recognise the political importance of popular sentiments and demands, however irrational or misguided they may be; but that does not justify him in endorsing such sentiments or supporting such demands. To do so would be to abandon leadership for demagogy. It would be following not leading opinion. The advocate of reason may, perhaps, under-estimate the force of "emotional currents," but full recognition of their power does not release him from his obligation to attempt to guide, to control, and, if need be, to divert them.

There is one aspect of the demand for action as such which deserves special comment, viz.: the popularity which the conception of authoritative large-scale long-period "planning" has acquired in recent years. Nearly everyone talks about "planning," but few have troubled as yet to enquire what is really involved in the notion of a "planned economy." We are not concerned here with the arguments for and against economic planning presented by those who have given serious thought to the subject; nor with the question whether or not a "planned economy" is consistent with the maintenance of democratic methods and institutions. We readily recognise that many people attracted by the idea of "planning" have no desire whatever to depart from the methods of parliamentary democracy. There are others, however, and it is with them that we are concerned. "Moscow has a Plan." The mere fact has had a wide appeal. The plan may be a good one or a bad one, but that is a minor detail. The fact is that there is a Plan, and that it is being vigorously, and even ruthlessly, enforced. For many people, it is the dictatorial imposition that provides the attraction, as much or more than the expected or actual results. What is wanted is drastic regimentation of everything and everybody, for its own sake. "Scratch a would-be 'planner'," it has been said, "and you find a would-be dictator." There is another side to the matter. Scratch some of the ordinary enthusiasts for "planning" and you find people who are merely anxious to escape from their democratic responsibilities.

9. *Political Zealotry*

The desire to enforce policies or changes upon others; the advocacy of revolutionary policies, on one side or the other, for which consent is clearly not obtainable; concentration upon ends at the expense of indifference to means; the demand for action as such; all constitute dangers to our system of parliamentary government.

There is, moreover, an attitude, associated in greater or less degree with all of them, which is entirely alien to democracy. That is the refusal to entertain the possibility of doubt as to the soundness of opinions held and policies advanced, and, therefore, the refusal to discuss and to seek accommodation with others. Many people hold their political views as religious dogmas, matters of faith rather than opinion, outside the scope of rational discussion. The spirit of fanaticism and self-righteousness is sometimes carried to such an extreme that there is a refusal to engage in friendly intercourse with opponents, or to tolerate such intercourse in others. To such people, compromise is ruled out, and moderation is regarded as a sin. Clearly, this is the antithesis of the democratic spirit. "I would," said Cromwell, "we should all take heed of mentioning our own thought and conceptions with that which is of God." "I know a man may answer all difficulties with faith, and faith will answer all difficulties really where it is," but "we are very apt all of us to call that faith which perhaps may be but carnal imagination and carnal reasonings." It is essential to democracy, to use Cromwell's words, that people "should not meet as two contrary parties, but as some desirous to satisfy and convince each other." Not long since, Professor Tawney urged the desirability of a party of "zealots," "Ironsides" and "Puritans." He wanted a New Model Socialist Party, a kind of religious sect, composed of men and women who "put socialism first, and whose creed carries conviction, because they live in accordance with it."[1] Such a party, we gather, would remain out of office until it comprised a majority of the electorate—the mere approval of a majority would not be good enough—

[1] "The Choice before the Labour Party," *The Political Quarterly*, July-September, 1932.

and would then proceed to act in strict accordance with its principles, i.e. to apply at once "fundamental," uncompromising, pure-and-undefiled, socialist measures. "The revolution" thus to be accomplished, be it noted, would be "peaceful." Mr. Tawney may legitimately be reminded of this country's previous experience of the "Rule of the Saints."

CHAPTER VI

THE CONDITIONS OF CONTINUANCE (II)

1. *The Necessity of Compromise*

ONE of the strongest appeals made by extremists,
and by all who are impatient of democratic conditions,
is that for "action in accordance with principles,"
and for "refusal to compromise." It is, perhaps, the
most popular criticism of the British system and
methods of government that "principles" are at a
discount, and that politicians are a thoroughly unprincipled set of people. The demand is for men who
will adhere unswervingly to their convictions. The
notion, apparently, is that people should formulate
or accept certain political principles, and then refuse
to agree to any action which is not in strict conformity
with such principles. They should not compromise
under any circumstances. There are, indeed, strange
"democrats" about who regard compromise as the
root of all political evil.

Yet, in refusing to compromise, people would be
rejecting one of the essential principles of democracy.
They may act in accordance with *their* principles, and,
up to a point, their principles may be sound; but,
obviously enough, they would not comprise the
principles of democratic action. From the democratic
standpoint, therefore, their principles would be
defective. This point is crucial.

148

The democratic method involves the determination of political principles as a result of discussion. The person or party formulating political principles or policies in advance of discussion and refusing to compromise under any circumstances; or settling such principles or policies before the process of discussion is completed, and refusing to compromise further; renders discussion a farce in the first case, and in the second limits its usefulness. The democratic method also involves the search for agreement through discussion, and action on the basis of the greatest possible measure of agreement obtainable. A compromise, of course, is only a settlement by mutual concessions, and, in practice, any agreement involves a measure of compromise.

Compromise has to be distinguished, of course, from the genuine accord which may emerge from discussion. Agreement may represent the general consensus of opinion after discussion, or it may be reached by concessions, but, as a rule, it represents a combination of both elements. Compromise, therefore, far from being the source of political immorality, is, from the democratic standpoint, one of the cardinal political virtues.

Lord Balfour said that if people "know not how to compromise and when," then "the successful working of British institutions may be difficult or impossible." "Problems of compromise," wrote Lord Morley, "are of the essence of the parliamentary and Cabinet system." No political party (save perhaps Professor Tawney's "Ironsides") can be formed without compromise. None can function within a democratic framework (not even Professor Tawney's) without it.

M

Any Cabinet represents to some extent a compromise, and its decisions are more often than not the result of compromise. Majority and minority alike are themselves based largely upon compromise, and the compromise between them secured and necessitated by their interchange of positions is only the last stage of a long series and forms a starting point for a new series. The process is continuous.

An uncompromising politician is an obstructive factor in democratic politics. He is, in fact, "impossible" in such conditions, and probably impossible under any conditions. Adamant against concessions, and also, as a rule, impervious to argument and persuasion, he is tolerated, indeed, only because his influence can be neutralised.

"What is wanted above all things in the business of joint counsel, is the faculty of making many one, of throwing the mind into the common stock."

So Gladstone said of Cabinet and parliamentary life.[1] Democracy is a business of joint counsel, and continental experience provides many illustrations of the fact that an uncompromising party, a non-co-operating party, is a source of weakness to any parliamentary system, and, if powerful, may well lead to its breakdown.

Many will concede the legitimacy of compromise on minor points, while asserting that there must be no compromise on essentials, but it is precisely in regard to what are considered essentials that compromise is called for, and is, indeed, imperative if

[1] *The Speaker*, Nov. 29th, 1890.   Quoted in Morley's *Life*, Book II, c. 6.

democratic institutions are to function. If Conservatives were to refuse to have any "truck" with "Socialism," or if they were to oppose an uncompromising negative to the Indian demand for self-government, then the continuance of democratic government would be impossible. The "Die-Hards" brought parliamentary institutions almost to a state of deadlock, and might even have precipitated civil war, in regard to the Irish claim for self-government, because they refused to compromise until it was too late. If the Liberals, regarding Free Trade as the Ark of the Covenant, were to decline to accept under any form any departure from the sacred principles, they, too, in certain circumstances, might seriously endanger the continuance of democratic methods. If it is true, as Professor Laski suggests, that, for the Labour Party, there can be no compromise with "capitalism," then the continuance of the Labour Party would involve the collapse of democratic government.[1] It may be noted that Sir Stafford Cripps proclaims his support of "truly democratic" methods, and at the same time declares that "there can and must be no compromise on essentials."

A man who enters into a compromise, it should be added, does not by so doing abandon his political aims. In the light of those aims, he makes, or endeavours to make, the best terms possible in the circumstances.[2] He does not put his policy into cold

---

[1] A Labour Party dictatorship would still necessitate "compromise with capitalism," unless a new age of miracles dawned upon us.

[2] Professor Laski assumes (*Democracy in Crisis*, pp. 261–3) that it must mean indefinite postponement of the issues, which is not the case. This assumption is the consequence of his view that there can be no compromise on certain questions.

storage; he secures the adoption of as much of it as he can, and may then resume his struggle for the rest. It is the non-compromiser whose policies are consigned permanently to the refrigerator: he, truly, is nothing but "a man of principles," for he does nothing effective to secure their adoption or application. Compromise, it is true, involves a modification of aims and policies at some point. In a compromise, or series of compromises, one side or the other, or both, must eventually renounce its original position, in fact if not in form. That is the inevitable corollary of the process. There may be nothing "unprincipled" involved unless any departure from one's original position is held to be unprincipled. If that is the case, then one side is bound to be "unprincipled," but, in fact, the denunciators of compromise do not regard concessions by their opponents as coming within that category. They would not regard as unprincipled even complete surrender by their opponents; for that would merely constitute a legitimate recognition of error. All are prepared to argue that the other fellow should compromise, even to the point of surrender, but there is very considerable reluctance to recognise that the process must be mutual.[1]

[1] It is granted that there are forms of compromise which it is difficult to defend. Writing from the progressive standpoint, Lord Morley has attempted to draw a distinction between legitimate and illegitimate kinds of compromise. "It may mean the deliberate suppression or mutilation of an idea, in order to make it congruous with the traditional idea or the current prejudice on the given subject, whatever that may be. Or else it may mean a rational acquiescence in the fact that the bulk of your contemporaries are not yet prepared either to embrace the new idea, or to change their ways of living in conformity to it. In the one case, the compromiser rejects the highest truth, or dissembles his own acceptance of it. In the other, he holds it courageously for his ensign and device, but neither forces nor expects the whole world straightway to follow.

Compromise, of course, does not mean the surrender of one side to the other. Both parties must make some contribution. Up to a point, the agreement may represent a genuine accord which has developed out of the controversy. Beyond that point, the contributions made by each side will depend, in the main, upon the respective strength of the parties at any given period of time. Still less does compromise involve surrender to threats of forcible action or resistance. It may be asserted, also, that insistence upon the necessity of compromise as a condition of the smooth functioning of parliamentary government does not imply that a party in power ought to do anything, or that an opposition party ought to acquiesce in anything, however contrary it may be to its general policy, merely for the sake of avoiding trouble. There are limits to compromise, but they must not be determined in advance by reference to "principles": they have to be discovered and determined in relation to the particular circumstances. It is in regard to compromise that many of the most serious practical problems of democracy arise. It is here that the democratic statesman encounters his chief difficulties. The

---

The first prolongs the duration of the empire of prejudice. and retards the arrival of improvement. The second does his best to abbreviate the one, and to hasten and make definite the other, yet he does not insist on hurrying changes which, to be effective, would require the active support of numbers of persons not ripe for them. It is legitimate compromise to say: 'I do not expect you to execute this improvement, or to surrender that prejudice, in my time. But at any rate it shall not be my fault if the improvement remains unknown or rejected. There shall be one man at least who has surrendered the prejudice, and who does not hide the fact.' It is illegitimate compromise to say: 'I cannot persuade you to accept my truth; therefore I will pretend to accept your untruth.' "—*On Compromise*, pp. 118–9. It is partly due to a failure to make this kind of distinction that so many people dislike the idea of compromise.

immediate point, however, is that a refusal to compromise on one side or the other imperils, in greater or less degree, any democratic system of government, and that any decision to reject a possible compromise must be taken in the light of that fact.

2. *Party Co-operation*

One corollary of the democratic process of compromise is that the minority party or parties must be prepared to accept the responsibilities of government. That is perfectly clear under two-party conditions, but it is not adequately appreciated when those conditions are absent. In the latter circumstances, no party is entitled to repudiate its share of responsibility for the conduct of government. Real responsibility cannot in fact be avoided, even by refusal to participate in the formation of a ministry, and no party is justified in taking up the attitude that it will not under any circumstances participate in office unless it has a majority of its own. In practice, such a policy weakens and may destroy parliamentary government. Evidence of the truth of this contention may be drawn from continental experience. The policy of non-collaboration in government with "capitalist" or "bourgeois" parties, long favoured and pursued by the socialistic parties in Europe, has been a great source of weakness to parliamentary institutions. It had to be abandoned by the German Social Democratic Party in its attempt to preserve the democratic republic. The French Socialist Party, also, has been compelled at times to modify its traditional attitude on the question; but its reluctance to do so, and the repeated reversions to its previous standpoint, have been a disturbing factor in the politics of the Third Republic, and a disintegrating force in the party itself.[1] The indications are that the exigencies of democratic government may compel the abandonment of its non-participation policy. They have already compelled the abandonment of the general policy of non-collaboration, for no essential difference exists, clearly enough, between socialist support of a "bourgeois" government (and electoral pacts with "bourgeois" parties) and socialist participation in a coalition government. The refusal of the latter, largely as a symbol of the "fundamental" distinctiveness of a Socialist Party, is, nevertheless, exasperating in its unfairness to the other party or parties concerned. Under three-party or multi-party conditions, no party can legitimately claim that it is free to repudiate direct governmental responsibility unless it has a majority over all other parties combined and is "free to carry out its own policy."[2] Obviously, this applies as much to the relinquishment as to the assumption of office.[3]

[1] The split in the French Socialist Party in November of 1933, leading to the formation of the new "Socialist Party of France" under MM. Renaudel and Marquet, is but the latest of a series which the Party has suffered owing to its attitude on this matter. It was the outcome of the successive refusals by the Party to allow members to accept ministerial posts in the Radical-Socialist Cabinets of MM. Herriot, Paul-Boncour, and Daladier, and the successive defeats of those ministries as a consequence of withdrawal of the Party's support. The Party has to bear a large part of the responsibility for the failure to provide a stable government of the Left in the present Chamber, and for the serious political crisis which developed.

[2] See below, pp. 226–9, for a discussion of the controversy in the British Labour Party on the question of "Minority government."

[3] It has been argued in defence of the Labour Party's actions during the crisis of 1931 that a Government is fully entitled, even under conditions in which no party has a clear majority and an

3. *Community versus Sectional Interests*

The multiplicity of parties and groups in certain
States is a sign that the spirit of co-operation and
compromise is inadequately developed. Few things
have done more to bring Continental democracies
into disrepute than the instability of ministries and
the repeated and often prolonged ministerial crises
resulting from the failure to secure effective co-operation between the political parties. The consequent

---

appeal to the electorate is undesirable, to decline to take action
which is opposed to its general policy and principles, and to resign.
A point may be reached, it is urged (and we think soundly urged)
at which a Government is justified in saying, "We cannot do
these things: if they must be done, then others must do them;
in so far as it is true that they are necessary, they are things for
which we are not responsible; and for which we cannot assume
responsibility." The contention is that, in the circumstances which
then existed, a Conservative-Liberal coalition could have taken
office and dealt with the situation which had arisen. Suppose,
however, that the Liberal Party or the Conservative Party also
refused to share in the responsibilities of government on similar
grounds. Clearly, if either or both had done so, deadlock would
have resulted. The attitude of the Labour Party on this occasion
constituted, in our view, a refusal to accept the implications of
democratic government. It might have fulfilled them, substantially,
by refraining from opposition to the measures proposed. This,
however, it refused to do. No one party, in such circumstances,
is entitled to say, "We must be allowed to deal with this matter
in our own way, or we shall not deal with it at all and shall oppose
any other body of people who attempt to deal with it," unless the
party concerned recognises, and is willing to face, the risks to
democratic government involved.

It is contended, however, that the actual position in 1931 was
that the Conservative and Liberal Parties *were* prepared to assume
governmental responsibility. If that had not been the case, it is
admitted that the Labour Party would have been obliged to act
differently. The implication is that, in such circumstances, the
Labour Party would have been prepared to accept the responsibility which they in fact repudiated. From the democratic standpoint, however, that does not exonerate the Labour Party, for
the argument implies that, just because the other parties were
willing to deal with the situation, the Labour Party was able to
take advantage of the opportunity to protect its partisan interests
by evading its share of responsibility.

feebleness of the executive has seriously undermined governmental efficiency. The plain lesson of recent happenings is that if people and parties are unwilling to collaborate and to compromise the requisite measure of unity will be imposed, sooner or later, by dictatorial methods. The supremacy of the community interest over all partial interests is no less necessary in the democratic State than in the "totalitarian" State of the Nazis or the Fascists: the difference between them relates to the methods of attaining that supremacy.

Party rigidity is one of the most potent forces making for dictatorship, and another is the constant bickering to which parties are only too prone. The temptation to make party capital out of unavoidable occurrences or out of necessary but unpalatable legislation is strong, and needs to be sternly resisted. Obstruction, in Parliament or elsewhere, is clearly contrary to the democratic method. Just as a majority party is under the obligation to take the wishes of the minority into consideration, so a minority party is under the obligation to co-operate as fully as possible with the government of the day. It is not the duty of an Opposition to oppose for the sake of opposition; rather is it its duty to agree wherever agreement is possible. The inevitable differences of opinion and interest in society are numerous and complex enough: they should not be complicated by disagreements manufactured in order to promote temporary party interests.

In the sphere of international relations, these considerations are of peculiar importance. In that sphere, the democratic method of patient striving for agreement by discussion and compromise is the only alternative to war. There are queer "democrats" who jeer at international conferences. They are probably, at best, people who identify democracy with "majority rule," but in international affairs it is clear that majority decisions, even if formally accepted, could not be effectively implemented if they represented merely the imposition of the will of a majority of governments upon the rest. It is difficult enough, as experience has shown, to secure the effective implementation of decisions generally agreed by governments. That is largely because the conditions of, as well as the need for, action in the international sphere are not adequately understood, and partly also because partisan advantage is taken of the limitations they impose upon the governments concerned. When most of the major problems of the day are international in scope, when none of them can be dealt with successfully on a purely domestic basis, it is essential to a continuance of parliamentary institutions that these defects should be remedied. The continuity of policy roughly secured under British parliamentary government is in no respect more necessary than in matters affecting international relations. The moderate oscillations resulting from changes in government, relatively harmless in domestic matters, may constitute a seriously disturbing factor in regard to international politics, and in this sphere, therefore, the fullest possible co-operation between the parties is especially desirable.

If parliamentary government is to function satisfactorily, it is clear also that where sectional interests of any kind come into conflict with the well-being of the community as a whole, they should be subordinated. One of the greatest problems of modern politics arises from the developed organization of sectional interests, which has assumed a great variety of forms. These interests, so far from providing the basis of party activities, often cut across them. Legislation in recent years has increasingly tended to take the form of bargaining between conflicting organized interests, in which the politician has acted as a go-between. Consultation of interests affected by proposed legislation is eminently desirable, but the supremacy of the general interest must be maintained. In so far as parties allow their activities to be dictated or diverted by powerful group interests, whether Employers' Associations, financial corporations, Trade Unions, religious bodies, organized industries or professions, or what not, they are failing to perform their proper functions in a democratic system of government.

Those who guide the day-to-day activities of the political parties have special responsibilities in these respects, but individuals generally have to recognise that they ought to put their duties as citizens first and foremost, their loyalty to the community above any lesser loyalties. As members of parties, they have to remember that a party is not an end in itself, but a means to an end, and that end the well-being of the community. That constitutes the essential justification for the existence of parties. Irrational adherence to a party, whatever it may do or propose, is an outstanding defect of political practice under parliamentary government.

A great deal of nonsense, undoubtedly, is talked about putting the nation before party. The phrase easily becomes a mere weapon in the conflict of parties. None the less, it has a real meaning, and can be legitimately used. In so far as a party is endeavouring to promote what it conceives to be the common good, then, of course, there is no question of it putting its own interests before those of the community. No party, it almost goes without saying, is moved solely by concern for the common good; no party is what an ideal party would be. Personal, sectional, class interests enter in, sometimes consciously, sometimes, indeed, avowedly, and very often subconsciously. Self-deception is proverbially easy. We all have a tendency to identify our own interests with the public welfare, and it is easy for a party to deceive itself, and to identify sectional or class interests of its members with the common good. However, all parties are, in some measure, moved by a desire to promote the common good, and all, in some measure, are mistaken in their views about what constitutes the common good. It is quite safe to say that no party has a monopoly of insight in that respect, just as no party has a monopoly of zeal for the public welfare. There is a natural tendency, of course, for all of us to think that we alone are animated by public spirit, and a natural temptation for us to think that our political opponents are animated by selfish motives. As everybody's opponents *are* animated by selfish motives to some extent, we can always confirm what we feel must be true about our opponents —and they about us. When the common good demands some personal sacrifice from us, we are all tempted, similarly, to assert that the sacrifice is not in the true interests of the community. When the sacrifice is demanded from others, and does not seem to affect us, directly or indirectly, we are apt to take a rather high line about the selfishness or lack of patriotism of any persons concerned who may raise objections.

At the same time, circumstances may arise in which a party deliberately takes a line which it knows is contrary to the public interest in order to advance or safeguard its own prospects. It will be generally agreed, for instance, that a change of circumstances may make it necessary or desirable for a party government to take action which would not be the sort of action normally taken by that government. Similarly, a party not forming the government may be called upon to support measures of a different kind from those it would otherwise have advocated, measures less directly conducive to the achievement of the general objects it may have in view. If either party, in such circumstances, refrains from taking the action it recognises ought to be taken, in order, say, to protect certain sectional interests, or to improve its electoral position, or to maintain unity in its ranks, then that party may justifiably be accused of placing its party fortunes before the national interests. It will be admitted that, whatever the party situation may be, circumstances may develop in which specially urgent matters have to be dealt with in order to safeguard the welfare of the community as a whole. If the action rendered necessary happens to be unpalatable to a particular party, and, just because it is unpalatable, the party declines to take that action, or opposes the action being taken, then again it may justly be held guilty of giving preference to party rather than community interests. It may be that the measures regarded as necessary are not so regarded by some members of the party. It may be that, distasteful as the measures are, many members of the party are willing to take or to support them. But if those who recognise that they ought to be taken oppose their being taken, because, for instance, of the risks to party unity involved, they, again, are guilty of putting party before the nation. They may hold that by preserving party unity they are, in the long run, acting in the best interests of the nation, since their party's aims are in the best interests of the nation, but, on the assumptions stated, they cannot escape the charge of sacrificing the immediate interests of the community as a whole to their special party interests. That may be, in certain circumstances, a grave charge. If a party takes advantage of an emergency situation to force through one of its party proposals, it may render itself liable to a similar charge. It may be, of course, that the particular proposal is helpful in the immediate situation, or it may be that the party concerned sincerely believes that the particular measure it advocated before the situation arose will be beneficial in the situation that has arisen. In so far as this is so, the party cannot be accused of putting its interests before the nation's, unless, perhaps, it takes action in order to get the particular item of policy applied, which itself prejudices the successful handling of the emergency. Admittedly, then, it is not easy to substantiate a charge that a political party is acting in opposition to what is clearly in the national interests. That the charge may be difficult to prove does not mean, however, that the accused party is not guilty. Parties may, and sometimes do, behave in that way, and when they do, their behaviour is a violation of the democratic method.

4. *Scope for Leadership*

Yet another important condition of the continuance of our political system is the maintenance of wide discretionary powers for representatives, for ministers or leaders of parliamentary parties, and for the Prime Minister or party chief. Attempts to transform the representative into the delegate of a party committee, or, still worse, into the paid servant of a particular interest; to bind parliamentary parties by conference decisions; to impose controls upon them from outside Parliament; to extort pledges and impose mandates; to fetter appointed leaders; indeed, all attempts to impose rigid disciplines from below; are fatal to representative democracy, and democracy, of course, must work through representatives.

The democratic process of seeking agreement through discussion and compromise is nullified if it is cut off before the crucial stages are reached, or rendered ineffective in those stages. Confidence in the representative and the leader is an essential element in parliamentary government. It has its corollary: the representative or the leader must take his public into his confidence. In these days, when the tasks of government are so complex, and when international questions are of such vital importance, it is more than ever the duty of the politician to interpret the situation, to "educate his masters," and to be honest and courageous in doing so. Efforts to limit the discretionary power of representatives arise largely, no doubt, from lack of confidence; yet where a lack of confidence exists, it casts a grave reflection upon those who have made the selections, upon those who are lacking in confidence. At the present time, there is a widespread mistrust of political representatives and leaders. The suggestion may be made that it is largely due to inadequate understanding, and not so much as is commonly supposed to the delinquencies of politicians. In view of recent happenings at home and abroad, it is difficult to avoid the conclusion that statesmen in every country are constantly hampered and sometimes thwarted by the prejudices and ignorances of the peoples to whom they are responsible. That this is, perhaps, less the case in this country than elsewhere is a hopeful sign for the future of British parliamentary government. Politicians, no doubt, cannot escape some measure of responsibility. They are too prone to give pledges; too anxious to prove their consistency; somewhat too fearful of taking an an unpopular course or of alienating influential groups; and too deficient in frankness. Too few representatives speak to their constituents and party committees in the language of Burke.

The most striking form taken by attempts to impose restrictions upon elected persons—made, with typical confusion, in the name of "democratic control"—is that of extra-parliamentary control exercised either by a party caucus or by a sectional organisation. Dangerous in the case of a parliamentary Opposition, it becomes disastrous when exercised in relation to a party in office. The evil has been seen at its worst, perhaps, in Australia,[1] but tendencies of the same sort have developed in this country, most noticeably in connection with the Labour Party.

There have been proposals to reserve important decisions either to the non-parliamentary Executive of the Party, to the National Joint Council (representing that Executive, the Parliamentary Party Executive and the General Council of the Trades Union Congress), or to the Labour Party in Conference assembled.[2] Suspicions have been aroused as to the measure of control exercised, or attempted, by the General Council of the Trades Union Congress over the actions of the party both in opposition and in office. Counter-charges have been made that the Conservative Party is subject to analogous influences or controls, though, in this case, clearly enough, there is not the same degree of formal association between the party and other bodies. Whatever the facts may be, any

[1] See Sir Harrison Moore's analysis of recent events in Australia, *Quarterly Review*, April, 1933.

[2] The Labour Party Conference at Hastings, October, 1933, adopted a Report submitted by the Executive Committee on "Labour and Government" which represents a partial acceptance of such proposals. While the Report leaves the final decision as to acceptance of office after a General Election in the hands of the Parliamentary Party, that body, in making its decision, is to have before it the recommendations of the National Joint Council, and, in the event of the Party being in a minority, the recommendations of a Special Conference of the Party at which the National Joint Council would attend. Similarly, the Report leaves the final responsibility for Ministerial appointments with the Labour Prime Minister, but he is to act in consultation with three elected members of the Parliamentary Party and the Secretary of the Labour Party. The Prime Minister, moreover, is to be subject to majority decisions of the Cabinet, and is only to recommend a Dissolution on the decision of the Cabinet confirmed by a Parliamentary Party meeting. More significant is the provision that the General Council of the Trades Union Congress is to be consulted in respect to the Sessional programme of the Parliamentary Party, and fully consulted with regard to proposed legislation in which it is directly concerned.

N

measure of control, formal or informal, exercised over parliamentary parties by extra-parliamentary bodies vitiates the democratic process.

The danger is particularly serious when the control exercised is of a financial nature. One of its by-products deserves special mention. The direct financing of candidates and members of Parliament by industrial or professional associations not only facilitates the kind of control referred to, but has a baneful influence upon the quality of our parliamentary personnel. Nowadays, for example, the existence of Trade Union "pocket-boroughs" is notorious, and it will be generally conceded that the compensatory benefit attributed in former days to the aristocratic patronage of youthful talent is conspicuously absent in the case of the Trade Unions. This factor operates to some extent in all the political parties, and, in the case of the Conservative Party, the quality of parliamentary representatives is impoverished by undue financial demands upon prospective candidates, and sometimes by an undemocratic process of selection.[1]

[1] See an article by the Hon. Quintin Hogg in *The Nineteenth Century*, January, 1934, in which the writer gives three examples. "The first case is a London constituency—a safe Tory seat. Selection of candidates (unless the rules have been altered very recently) is by the executive committee, the general body of the association having no power of suggestion, but only a right of veto. Membership of the executive committee can be obtained by a subscription of £5 annually, which gives the subscriber a right to a seat upon this body and to the title and style of vice-president of the association. The second case is an agricultural constituency in the Eastern Counties. Again the seat may be regarded as safe for Conservatism. Until recently it was held by an extremely wealthy man. Prospective Conservative candidates have been informed that they need not apply unless they subscribe to the local association the fantastic sum of £3,000 per annum. The third example is of a safe Conservative seat in the residential area of a northern industrial city. Prospective candidates for Parliament have been informed that £600 a year is the least annual subscription which the association will consider."

5. " *The Inevitability of Gradualness* "

The continuance and smooth functioning of our political system are dependent upon the recognition and acceptance of the democratic method and its implications. Freedom of discussion, and freedom of political association (save for overtly subversive purposes) are obviously indispensable. The policies of governments must be such that they will have the support or acquiescence of virtually the whole community. A Government should act so far as it possibly can on behalf, not merely of its majority, but of the opposing minority or minorities as well. It must recognise that it cannot impose just what it likes upon the rest of the community, particularly if it is a government desirous of effecting important changes.

A Government must endeavour to meet the wishes and criticisms of the minority, because a high degree of continuity is essential; the system cannot stand the strain of sudden breaks and drastic oscillations in policy. That fact imposes a severe restraint not only upon the practice of repeal but also upon the general use of majority powers. It follows that policies must be appropriate to, and adapted to changes in, the circumstances. Parties desirous of effecting far-reaching changes in society must recognise, therefore, the "inevitability of gradualness" both in their formulation of practical programmes and in their attempted application of them.

This much-misunderstood phrase is not so much a declaration of policy as the statement of a fact. It does not mean deliberately "going slow" when it is possible to go fast, but simply that, whatever the pace, changes under democratic conditions must be gradual, i.e. they must proceed by steps or stages. That is true of all change, obviously enough, but the methods of parliamentary democracy impose the condition that the successive steps must be approved by the majority of the community and freely acquiesced in by the remainder. The "inevitability of gradualness" does not imply that sweeping changes are impossible of accomplishment by democratic methods. It does not imply that their gradual accomplishment must of necessity be slow. The speed of change is dependent upon the will of the community, and the speed limit is variable. Changes which are regarded as intolerable in one given set of circumstances may be generally welcomed in another. What *is* ruled out, in practice, is anything in the nature of an abrupt "revolutionary change in our whole social system."

There are some democrats who contend that parliamentary democracy can be speeded up to such an extent that decisions can be taken as rapidly as under dictatorships. That, in our view, is a delusion. Democratic government must be comparatively slow in the taking of decisions: that is the price which has to be paid for political freedom. It is true that in times of emergency extensive powers of immediate action may be conferred upon governments under democratic conditions. That has often been done, and it is important to note that the position thus created is very different from that under dictatorship. The expression "temporary dictatorship" is often applied to such a situation, but it is, in fact, misleading, for free discussion and criticism continues, the use made of emergency powers granted may be effectively challenged, and the powers themselves, if necessary, withdrawn. Nevertheless, a partial abrogation of the methods of democracy is involved, and the situation, however necessary, is, from the democratic standpoint, regrettable.

It does not follow, however, that democratic action is necessarily slower than dictatorial action. The taking of decisions is one thing, and lasting achievement quite another. Most dictators spend a great deal of their time in reversing or modifying their own decisions. Decree follows decree in bewildering succession, and with much repetition. Moreover, while the dictator may be able to act swiftly when his mind is made up, it does not follow that he can make up his mind with the same celerity. Is there no hesitation under dictatorial government, no divided counsel, no muddled and inconsistent action? More important, the achievements of dictatorships are relatively unstable precisely because of the methods employed. In so far as they are permanent, they could be secured as well or better by the democratic method. In judging the relative speed of the alternative methods, it is unsafe to take a short-run view. The energy of dictatorships may be imposing for a while, but account has to be taken of the special difficulties which dictatorships create for themselves, and of the inevitable reactions to policies which are not based upon voluntary agreement.

6. *Political Education*

Underlying the whole problem of maintaining and improving parliamentary government is the problem of political education. It has rightly been said that democracy would be a sham "if the votes of the electors were no more than the expression of blind mass emotion, itself directed and manipulated by purposeful vapourings in the Press, by seductive orators on the platform, or by specious appeals to class interest or individual greed." The vital importance of this aspect of the matter is generally conceded, and yet relatively little has been done in recent years to remedy the defects which obviously exist.

The problem is too large for adequate consideration here, but a number of points may usefully be made. It is widely accepted that the success of any system of parliamentary government is largely conditional upon the general standard of education in the community concerned. The improvement of our educational system as a whole is, therefore, urgently necessary; and it is particularly desirable that there should be a far greater measure of equality in regard to opportunities for higher education than at present obtains. At the same time, the extension of general educational opportunities is not sufficient. What is wanted, throughout our educational system, is that greater attention should be paid to specifically political education. The effects of general education are indirect, and, though important, may easily be exaggerated. The lack of political intelligence displayed by so many people who have had access to the highest forms of education provides clear evidence of the fact. The majority of electors in University constituencies are certainly little better qualified to perform the duties of citizenship than other people. That is not wholly due to specialisation in other matters, or to lack of interest in politics. It is partly due to the fact that the majority of those who pass through the higher grades of our educational process have little or no education in the theory and practice of politics.

So far as the vast majority of citizens, who conclude their scholastic careers at the age of fourteen or fifteen, are concerned, the position is of course lamentable. No doubt, it is too much to expect that people generally, in any grade of society, will ever take a keen and continuous interest in politics; and it is doubtless impossible for most people to understand the manifold and increasingly complex political problems of the day. Indeed, it is clearly impossible for any individual to understand all such problems. Nevertheless, much can be done to improve the situation. It is reasonable to ask that adequate opportunities should be provided for all those who are anxious to improve their political knowledge and capacities. It is also reasonable to contend that all citizens ought to be sufficiently educated to understand the existing political system and how it has arisen, to distinguish between rational arguments and plausible appeals to prejudice and self-interest, and to exercise common-sense judgments upon the issues presented to them for decision.

With this object in view, the extension of the school-leaving age, desirable on several grounds, should be utilised to provide further elementary education in history, civics and economics.[1] The

---

[1] I do not mean to suggest that such education should be confined to lectures and book-reading. On the contrary, it is of the utmost importance that the habit of discussion should be developed, and opportunities afforded for the acquisition of practical experience of democratic methods.

curricula in secondary and Public schools, and in the Universities, should be revised to give greater attention to these matters, not only as specialised studies, but as part of the compulsory routine. Most important of all, the various agencies for providing adult education should be energetically promoted.

A great deal might be done in this direction by the political parties: much of their energy might be diverted, to their own advantage, from propagandist meetings to the training of their own members in serious study of political problems. It may be questioned whether such activities undertaken under party auspices would not still be propagandist rather than educational. That might well be so, but even if it were, something would be achieved if partisans had a better understanding of their own party's case. However, there must be people in all parties who do not think it enough, in Mill's words, "if a person assents undoubtingly to what they think true, though he has no knowledge whatever of the grounds of the opinion, and could not make a tenable defence of it against the most superficial objections," and who appreciate that "he who knows only his side of the case, knows little of that."[1] It is very desirable that such people should give a lead in promoting political education within their own parties.

The task of political education ought, no doubt, to be conducted on a non-party basis, but, in view of the suspicion which unfortunately exists that such education is "biassed," there is much to be said for supplementary (if less satisfactory) educational activities by the parties themselves. At the same time,

[1] *On Liberty*, pp. 45–6. (The World's Classics Edition.)

political education for adults on a non-party basis needs to be encouraged in every possible way. The democratic State should regard this as one of its indispensable functions. The best method of dealing with the problem would be an extension of the existing work of the Extra-Mural Departments of the Universities and of such bodies as the Workers' Educational Association. The provision of further facilities for this work is urgently required. On the other hand, much depends upon the attitude of the political parties to adult education. In the past, no party has given it the measure of support which ought to have been forthcoming from parties pledged to the democratic method. That, once again, is largely because that method has not been properly understood.

People generally are still too reluctant to hear and consider arguments which run counter to their own political opinions; in practice they still burke free discussion, however enthusiastic their verbal support of it may be. Mill's well-known criticism is valid yet for far too many:—

"Their conclusion may be true, but it might be false for anything they know: they have never thrown themselves into the mental position of those who think differently from them, and considered what such persons may have to say; and consequently they do not, in any proper sense of the word, know the doctrine which they themselves profess."[1]

It may be urged that the reluctance of parties to encourage adult education, and of individual partisans to take advantage of such opportunities as are avail-

[1] *Op. cit.*, p. 47.

able, is in large measure due to doubts about the
non-partisan character of such education. That there
are possible dangers of that kind in State control or
supervision of adult education may be granted; and
those with experience will readily admit the difficulties
of maintaining the desirable degree of impartiality.
But the criticisms sometimes levelled against the
existing system of adult education from this standpoint have an extremely slender basis in fact. The
freedom in teaching and the insistence upon, and
free expression of opinion in, discussion by students
provide adequate safeguards.[1] A Tutorial or other
Adult Class in which there are students drawn from
all political parties furnishes an admirable illustration
of the democratic process of discussion; and the
experience of the adult education movement in this
country has proved conclusively, if any proof is
required, that it is possible to attain a high degree
of impartiality in the study even of highly contro-
versial political problems.[2]

The real basis of opposition to adult education, in
so far as it is not mere ignorance, is to be found in a
preference for propaganda as opposed to education.
It is its impartiality, not its bias, which is objected to.
People of all parties are too inclined to argue that
"He who is not with us is against us." The criticisms
and suspicions of the parties cancel out in an amusing
and instructive manner, as in the case of criticisms
of the British Broadcasting Corporation. Parties show
too much anxiety to shield their members from
possible contamination by adverse facts or arguments.

[1] Similar criticisms of University education are equally unfounded.
[2] The admirable impartiality of the B.B.C. in its conduct of
political talks provides further evidence.

They fear that the statement and consideration of objections and difficulties may weaken the morale of the party and lead to uncertainty and inaction. In so far as anyone is influenced by such motives, he falls short of the democratic position. Mill, as usual, has given him the appropriate answer. "The steady habit of correcting and completing his own opinion by collating it with those of others, so far from causing doubt and hesitation in carrying it into practice, is the only stable foundation for a just reliance on it." [1]

[1] *Op. cit.*, p. 28.

PART TWO

RECENT TENDENCIES IN BRITISH POLITICS

"What do angry men ail to rail so against Moderation; doth it not look as if they were going to some very scurvy Extreme, that is too strong to be digested by the more considering part of Mankind? These arbitrary methods, besides the injustice of them, are (God be thanked) very unskilful too, for they fright the Birds, by talking so loud, from coming into the Nets that are laid for them; and when Men agree to rifle a House, they seldom give warning, or blow a Trumpet; but there are some small States-men, who are so full charg'd with their own Expectations, that they cannot contain. And kind Heaven by sending such a seasonable curse upon their undertakings, hath made their ignorance an Antidote against their Malice; some of these cannot treat peaceably; yielding will not satisfy them, they will have men by storm; there are others, that must have Plots, to make their Service more necessary, and have an Interest to keep them alive, since they are to live upon them. . . ."—HALIFAX.

1. *Introduction*

A CONSIDERATION of certain recent developments in British politics may illustrate and expand the case presented in the preceding chapters, and may serve to indicate more clearly some of the dangers which threaten British parliamentary government.

The future depends essentially upon the behaviour of the great political parties; primarily upon the Conservative and Labour Parties, secondarily upon the Liberal party or parties. To some minds it may seem that attention should be directed to those movements which, more or less frankly, reject parliamentary government; but such movements do not as yet constitute a serious threat to our institutions. The British Communist Party, and the Independent Labour Party (which has in recent years moved rapidly to an anti-parliamentary standpoint), are relatively unimportant: the Communist position, in any event, is well-known and needs no examination here. In the last year or so, the British Union of Fascists, under the leadership of Sir Oswald Mosley, has attracted considerable attention. As a political force it is as yet a largely unknown quantity, but it is rapidly ceasing to arouse amusement and beginning to cause alarm, probably more because of events abroad than because of its own activities. It will have to receive notice as a new phenomenon in British politics. However, our system of parliamentary government is far less likely to succumb to a direct challenge from new parties, either Communist or Fascist, than to betrayal, conscious or otherwise, by the established parties. Responsibility rests mainly upon the latter, and it is upon them that we must concentrate our attention.

In this respect, the more immediate dangers to the democratic political system seemed until recently to threaten from the Left rather than from the Right. That may appear to many people a paradoxical assertion, since Parties of the Left (the Communist Party excepted) are usually enthusiastic in their protestations of support for democracy. To assert that the actions or policy of the Labour Party contain elements of danger to democracy may appear to some minds to be paradoxical to the point of malice. None the less, the assertion can be substantiated. It is not suggested that the position has become serious; nor does consideration of the Labour Party's attitude from this standpoint imply that there are no potential dangers from other quarters. That is far from being the case. Indeed, in one important sense, the potential danger from the Right is much more serious, because, while a Party of the Left would have little chance of success in any attempt to destroy parliamentary institutions, an attempt to set up a Dictatorship of the Right might well be carried to a successful conclusion. However, we are concerned here with actions which may unintentionally endanger parliamentary government rather than with deliberate attempts to destroy it; and it is in the ranks of the Labour Party that disturbing tendencies first developed in recent years.[1] Ample evidence of the fact can be provided from official Labour sources.[2] There is

[1] "It is unfortunate that the first talk about dictatorship should be coming from the Labour ranks."—The Rt. Hon. H. B. Lees Smith, Speech at Preston, 24th June, 1933.

[2] See, e.g. *The Labour Magazine*, Official Journal of the Trades Union Congress and the Labour Party, June 1933.—"For many months past a singularly untimely and politically inept propaganda has been carried on by a non-official group, with the object, it would seem, of convincing the Labour Movement that the accomplishment of Socialism will probably be preceded by revolutionary violence and will certainly require the exercise of powers of dictatorship by a Socialist Government which means business. Lip service is paid in this propaganda to the ideals of democracy and the free institutions it has created, but they are regarded as milestones which have been passed on the road to freedom, and we need not trouble to go back to defend them. A Socialist dictatorship (they contend) will have to be set up, and it will have no more use for free speech and a free press, for the right of public assembly and the right of combination, for free elections and a free Parliament, than a Right dictatorship will have for them; in fact, as one of the spokesmen of the group put it, free speech is no more one of the eternal verities than free trade."

additional justification for giving priority of consideration in this matter to the Labour Party: in the first place, the Party is relatively new and relatively inexperienced; in the second place, while tendencies which are contrary to democratic action have received expression inside the Labour Party organisation, and even from prominent Labour M.P.'s and ex-Ministers, similar tendencies on the Right have not as yet disclosed themselves in the Conservative Party organisation, and have received no countenance from Conservative leaders and members of Parliament; and, finally, since the Labour Party is more given to talking aloud and blowing trumpets than its Conservative rival, it provides much more material for our illustrative purpose.

2. *The Labour Party's Rejection of "Gradualism"*

With regard to the Labour Party, it is readily admitted that the dangers are not realised, for the most part, by those concerned. There is little conscious desire to depart from the traditional British political methods. The trouble arises, essentially, from failure to grasp their implications, and a consequent reluctance to accept the limitations they impose. That is in part attributable to the confusion about "democracy" previously discussed, which makes it possible for a false distinction to be drawn between "democracy" and "our existing parliamentary methods."

The problems of political method have never been faced frankly by the British Labour Party as a whole. For the most part, the Party has merely assumed that its aims could be achieved by parliamentary methods, but, underlying the apparently general acceptance of such methods, important divergencies of view have always existed, and have recurrently come into the open. After the Party's accession to office in 1924, those divergencies widened. The conditions imposed by parliamentary democracy became more apparent, and revolt against them began to grow. Those who had led the Party, and had endeavoured to train it in British political methods, were subjected to a criticism which increased in volume and bitterness. The fall of the Labour Government in 1931, and the consequent breach in the party ranks, was due, primarily, to the fact that the Party was not agreed on questions of political method. It was the outcome of long-standing differences. These, however, did not correspond by any means to the actual alignment in 1931, for other factors entered into the respective decisions, and the divergencies remain in the Labour Party as at present constituted.

The exclusion of Mr. MacDonald and his avowed supporters has, of course, weakened those who are willing to accept the limitations of parliamentary methods. Indeed, those who have rejected or are impatient with such methods apparently dominated the Party's activities during the next eighteen months. Their supremacy was clearly seen at the Leicester Annual Conference of the Party in October, 1932. A complete severance from the methods of the past was the key-note of the proceedings. The position has been summed up by Professor H. J. Laski in these terms:—

"For the first time in its history the Labour Party was driven to recognise that compromise with capitalism was impossible. It adopted a policy of which the central purpose was a direct assault upon the foundations of economic power. . . . It proposed to use the normal mechanics of the constitution for its purposes; it was not, at least consciously, in any sense a revolutionary party. But the experience of 1931 led it deliberately to abandon its belief in 'the inevitability of gradualness.' It announced that the transference to the State of the key economic positions must immediately follow upon its next conquest of the electorate."[1]

It may be pointed out that the Party had never "conquered" the electorate, and that influential groups within the Party had always insisted that "compromise with capitalism" was impossible (i.e. undesirable), continuously denounced it, and rejected "the inevitability of gradualness." At the 1932 Conference, these groups won all along the line, and "gradualism" was renounced. Anything which savoured of it was promptly turned down; indeed, a speaker had only to apply the label to a project to ensure its rejection. There were to be no more half-measures.

3. *The Unofficial "Revolution by Constitutional Means"*

It is to be observed, however, that the Labour Party, in its renunciation of "gradualism," and its adoption of a policy of sudden and drastic socialist change, did not consciously abandon parliamentary methods. The criticisms of its former leaders had implied that such a policy could be carried out by such methods. One group of critics, however, were not so confident. Led by Mr. G. D. H. Cole and Professor Laski, and with Sir Stafford Cripps as their parliamentary mouthpiece, a body of intellectuals associated together in the

[1] *Democracy in Crisis*, p. 38.

Society for Socialist Information and Propaganda (subsequently merged in the Socialist League), proceeded to pour forth a spate of books, pamphlets, articles and speeches, in which "A Plan" was outlined for effecting "immediate, far-reaching and simultaneous changes affecting the entire social system."[1] The new policy was "designed immediately upon our coming into power to compass the taking over of the key institutions of Capitalism and their transference at a blow to complete Socialist control."[2] The "revolutionary" nature of this policy was frankly recognised,[3] and its advocates (whose unofficial position must not be forgotten), began seriously to consider whether a revolutionary policy could be carried out by any but revolutionary methods. Their answer is not devoid of ambiguity. They admit that the customary parliamentary methods cannot be adhered to.[4] It has already been seen that both Mr. Cole and Professor Laski insist that our system of government cannot continue to function if a party in office attempts "a complete change in the whole social system." On the other hand, they reject Communist methods. There is to be no attempt to seize the power of the

[1] G. D. H. Cole, *A Plan for Britain*, p. 37.

[2] Ibid. p. 8.

[3] "We are determined to use our return to power to make a 'revolution,' none the less because we hope to make it by non-violent and constitutional means."—Cole, p. 39.

"It would be much better to use the word 'revolutionary' freely and to frankly adopt that adjective for Labour Party policy, disregarding any fears that it may create."—The Rt. Hon. Sir Charles Trevelyan, *The Challenge to Capitalism*, p. 3.

[4] "The parliamentary machine, as it now exists, is . . . utterly unsuitable for our purpose."—Cole, *A Plan for Britain*, p. 37.

". . . it is no good pretending that Socialism can ever be accomplished by our existing Parliamentary methods."—Sir Stafford Cripps, *The News Chronicle*, June 22nd, 1933.

State by a coup d'état. The keenest anxiety is displayed to avoid any resort to violence on either side. The policy, accordingly, must be "neither purely parliamentary nor purely Communist."

"The third alternative" must be tried.[1] What is this third alternative? It is to attempt "a revolution by constitutional means."

"'Revolutionary action,' such as we have in mind, can be taken within the four walls of the Constitution; and it is our business to master the methods of doing this, so that, if lawlessness and unconstitutionality are to arise, they shall come, not from us, but from our opponents."[2]

In fact, only the forms of effecting constitutional changes are to be respected. Parliamentary methods, as we have known them, are to go. It is not a matter of making minor adjustments. The whole spirit of democratic practice is to be violated. It is not that Sir Stafford Cripps and his associates really desire to destroy democratic institutions: they are anxious only to carry out their revolutionary aims. Indeed, the notion of Sir Stafford as a possible British dictator is absurd: an accidental prominence has been given to his utterances owing to the electoral misfortunes of the Labour Party, and it is largely owing to his lack of political experience that his opponents have been able to transform him into a not very convincing bogie-man. Nevertheless, the effect of the policy referred to would be to set up a Socialist Party dictatorship under constitutional forms. It has been said that "the idea of waiting until the result of a General Election

---

[1] Cole, *The Intelligent Man's Guide through World Chaos*, p. 608.
[2] Cole, *A Plan for Britain*, pp. 39–40.

is absolutely the only trace of democracy in the whole plan."[1] The details of the plan, and the language in which it has been presented, justify the verdict.

The Labour Party, writes Professor Laski,

'would have to take vast powers and legislate under them by ordinance and decree; *it would have to suspend the classic formulæ of normal opposition.*"[2]

The Plan provides that, on assuming office, the Socialist Government would at once face Parliament, and insist upon the passage "through all its stages on the first day" of an Emergency Powers Bill, "wide enough in its terms to allow all that will be immediately necessary to be done by ministerial orders." The Bill would confer authority "at once to take over or regulate the financial machine and to take any measures the situation might require for the immediate control or socialisation of industry."[3] Subsequently, there would be an Annual Planning and Finance Bill. This would lay down the main lines of legislation in every sphere for the coming year or period of years, and, once decided upon, re-discussion of the merits of the plan would be barred. This Annual Bill would be passed under a time-table motion, and would take the place of "the King's Speech, the Budget, financial resolutions, and the second reading debate on most of the important measures during the year."[4]

[1] *The Times*, May 6th, 1933.
[2] *Democracy in Crisis*, p. 87.   My italics.
[3] "We shall have to assume the authority not only to take over the banks and other financial institutions, but also simply to commandeer any factory or industry that we need."—Cole, *A Plan for Britain*, p. 38.
[4] Sir Stafford Cripps, *Can Socialism come by Constitutional Methods?* p. 9.

Secondary legislation would have a short second reading stage, and one final stage for dealing with Government amendments alone. Only general principles and enabling powers, however, would be put into Acts of Parliament, "the details being filled in by Orders and Regulations made by the Government itself under the authority conferred by these General Acts."[1] The use of legislative powers delegated to the Government, therefore, would be made general, and, according to some versions, the sole right to challenge orders made in virtue thereof would rest with Parliament; the Courts would have no power in that respect. It may also be noted that "the formation of a government must be the work of the Party, and the Party must have the right at any time to substitute fresh ministers in the places of any they desire to recall." The Prime Minister would be placed on the same level as his Cabinet colleagues, and forbidden to tender personal advice to the King.

That serious difficulties are likely to arise if any attempt is made to follow this kind of procedure is fully recognised by its advocates. There is the problem of the House of Lords, which must pass the proposed Emergency Powers Act, to say nothing of subsequent legislation.

Therefore, "we ought to say to the King that we will not consent to take office, but will at once overthrow any alternative Government he may set up, unless he agrees in advance to our creating enough peers of our own not merely to overcome the Lords' opposition to any actual measure we may bring forward, but to carry at once a Bill abolishing the House of Lords once and for all."[2]

[1] Cole, *A Plan for Britain*, p. 38.
[2] Cole, *A Plan for Britain*, p. 39.

The Crown must, indeed, give a pledge that its prerogative will be at the Socialist Government's disposal to surmount all opposition to its plans.

The King, however, may refuse to give the desired guarantees, and another General Election may have to be contested. Moreover, the possibility of resistance cannot be ruled out, since "the very foundations of the régime would be in question." It may be necessary, therefore, for the Socialist Government to make itself temporarily into a dictatorship. And even if the Government overcame its initial difficulties, and proceeded to carry out its Five Year Plan, the question would then arise whether it could safely submit its achievements to the verdict of the electorate.

"A Labour Government, which meant what it says, and had the power to give it statutory force, could not, at least easily, see its measures repealed by a Conservative successor, and it is at least dubious whether the latter would be prepared to acquiesce in the denial of the law of its own being."

"If its policy met with peaceful acceptance, the continuance of parliamentary government would depend upon its possession of guarantees from the Conservative Party that its work of transformation would not be disrupted by repeal in the event of its defeat at the polls. Could such guarantees be given? Would they be implemented if they were?"[1]

The implication is obvious, and Sir Stafford Cripps does not hesitate to mention the possibility of "adopting some exceptional means such as the prolongation of the life of Parliament for a further term without an election."

[1] Laski, *Democracy in Crisis*, p. 83.

It is unnecessary to go further into details. The
"constitutional methods" are a mere camouflage for
dictatorship. They are adhered to from a genuine
desire to avoid violence and economic disaster. There
is, however, no assurance that these evils would be
avoided; on the contrary, it is clearly demonstrated
that they are almost bound to follow. Professor
Laski's *Democracy in Crisis* itself furnishes the most
crushing reply to the policy he advocates. He shows
that if one great party is determined to revolutionise
the economic and social structure in the manner proposed, then the chance of avoiding a breakdown of
parliamentary government, a revolutionary situation,
and a resort to dictatorship on one side or the other,
is extremely slender. That, indeed, is the main theme
of the book. Professor Laski assumes that the position
envisaged has actually arisen, or must very soon arise.
It is certainly a possibility, but the most striking thing
is that he is actively engaged in bringing it about.
The only glimmering of hope he is able to discern is
that the opponents of his Socialist Government will
acquiesce in the proposed revolution. That is what,
he contends, they ought, democratically, to do. We
are determined to have our own way, he argues in
effect, and it is the duty of others to let us have it:
the responsibility for any trouble which may arise
will rest upon them. Sir Stafford Cripps takes the
same line :—

"It is this complete severance with all traditional
theories of Government, this determination to seize power
from the ruling class and transfer it to the people as a
whole that differentiates the present political struggle
from all those that have gone before.

"The decisive blow at capitalism must be struck while the people's mandate is fresh and strong. That blow can be delivered constitutionally; if unconstitutional means are used to resist it, those who use unconstitutional means must not complain if they are met with force."[1]

"Unconstitutional," in British political terminology, has come to mean almost anything to which objection is taken. The answer to Sir Stafford is that those who depart from the customary British political methods have only themselves to blame for any consequences which may ensue. It is not altogether surprising that his policy is presented in the name of "democracy." It is only, on the more charitable view, another instance of the abuse of that "blessed word." Power, it will be noted, is to be transferred to "the people as a whole." Indeed, "the primary object is to preserve democracy, in the sense that *the people* through Parliament initiate the main lines of the National Plan and have power to see that it is carried out." Sir Stafford wants a "vigorous effective democracy . . . determined to express *its will* and see that will carried into effect."[2] His Socialist Government would, no doubt, exercise a "democratic dictatorship!"

Credit, however, must be given to this group of "intellectuals" for drawing attention by their propaganda to the implications of the abandonment of "gradualism." The more active they are in doing so, the less likelihood will there be of the Labour Party adhering to their "revolutionary policy," and the less likelihood, therefore, of a breakdown in British parliamentary government. The more it becomes apparent

[1] *Can Socialism come by Constitutional Methods ?*
[2] My italics.

that any attempt to carry out an abruptly drastic transformation of our economic and social structure involves the abandonment of our political institutions and methods, and the risk, amounting almost to a certainty, of a revolutionary situation, with all the consequences that may entail, the less willing people will be to proceed on those lines.

4. *The Reaction to the " Cripps " Proposals*

Already a strong reaction has set in, and grows steadily in power. It became discernible in the ranks of the Labour Party during the course of the year 1933, and was largely due to the alarm inspired by the fate which has befallen German Social Democracy and the German Trade Union Movement. It was also due to the realisation, after "Nazi" Revolution, of the full implications of the loss of political liberty involved in the rejection of parliamentary government. At the same time, the divergencies of view within the Labour Party must be remembered. The more moderate elements had remained in control of the central party machine and of the closely associated General Council of the Trades Union Congress. In the situation that had arisen, these elements, capably led by Mr. Walter Citrine, were able to strike an effective blow at the propaganda of the Socialist League by condemning all dictatorship and expressing opposition to any attempt to supersede Parliament or to undermine its democratic working; and at the same time to re-assert and consolidate their authority within the Labour Party and its connected organisations. The result has been a strong re-affirmation by the Labour Party and the Trades Union Congress of their adhesion to democracy and parliamentary government.[1]

Sir Stafford Cripps and his associates, placed at a corresponding disadvantage by the reaction to continental events, proceeded to tone down their utterances (and even their previous writings). Without abandoning their plans, they promptly denounced dictatorship, as vehemently as the rest, and asserted their belief in democracy and the attainment of Socialism by peaceful means. Disingenuously, they interpreted their proposals merely as an attempt to make parliamentary procedure more efficient and more "democratic."

The internal conflict in the Labour Party thus continues. The confusion has not been dispelled, for the simple reason that the central issue is still obscured. The essential point in the controversy is the nature of the policy it is proposed to pursue when power is acquired as the result of a General Election. Flirtation with the idea of dictatorship (however disguised) is the logical outcome of the "revolutionary

---

[1] See the Manifesto, "Democracy v. Dictatorship," issued by the National Joint Council, March 24th, 1933: and the Reports of the Trades Union Congress at Brighton (September, 1933) and of the Labour Party Conference at Hastings (October, 1933). It is true that the Labour Party Conference at Hastings avoided a direct decision on the Cripps proposals, which were referred to the National Executive Committee for consideration and report, but, if a decision had then been taken, it is almost certain that it would have been adverse. The Hastings procedure was adopted, no doubt, in order to avert an open breach in the Party. The proceedings of the next Annual Conference at Southport, October, 1934, show that in the interval the moderate leadership of the Party has further consolidated its position. Despite a preliminary blowing of trumpets, only "a sparse skeleton" (as Dr. Hugh Dalton described it) of the Cripps proposals was presented to the Conference, and that was decisively rejected.

policy" advocated by the intellectuals of the Socialist
League. On the other hand, the official moderates
hesitate as yet to adapt policy frankly to the requirements of their democratic creed, for they also are
(verbally) opposed to "gradualism."[1] It is true that
the official policy presented to the Annual Conference
at Southport (October, 1934), is based, in reality,
upon an acceptance of the fact of the "inevitability
of gradualness," and provides evidence of a recognition,
however incomplete, of the limitations of the democratic
method. The Labour Party has wheeled to the Right,
and "MacDonaldism" is once again in the ascendant.
Yet the full implications of the change have been
concealed by the retention, whenever possible, of the
militant phraseology of 1932. The Left-Wing
intelligentsia have considerable scope for plausible
interpretation of Conference decisions in senses convenient for furtherance of their purposes. They have
reverted to more subtle tactics, and it would be
premature to assume that their eventual defeat is
assured. Owing to their propaganda, the drive for a
"revolutionary policy" has become relatively strong.
It is based upon misunderstandings, and supported
by arguments, which merit further consideration.

5. "*Majority Rule*"

It is plain that the incompatibility of revolutionary
policy and democratic method is not yet fully
recognised. One reason for that is the assumption
that under democratic conditions a majority is entitled

---

[1] There are signs, however, in certain cases, notably those of
Mr. Citrine and Mr. Herbert Morrison, of a willingness to describe
the course they favour by the appropriate but suspect word.

to carry out its declared policy without let or hindrance or modification. If a Labour Government does not do what it is entitled to do, that is because, so it is suggested, either the leaders of the Party are lacking in boldness and sincerity, or its opponents use the political machinery or their economic power to obstruct the application of Labour policy and to bring about the downfall of the Government. Of course, there has not yet been a Labour Government with a Labour majority behind it, but, none the less, the argument has been applied to both Labour minority governments.

We have already seen that the identification of democracy with majority rule is not permissible. The "will of the majority" is not "the will of the people"; and the will of a party conference (itself expressed in majority decisions) is not the will of the majority. A Cabinet has to interpret, as best it can, "the will of the people." In this connection, Professor Laski has stated the necessary conditions of parliamentary government in terms with which we have no serious quarrel.

"In government by party . . . the Opposition takes office with the understanding that acceptance of its will by Parliament gives it the right to rule the country in accordance with its principles. Each party accepts, however much it may dislike, the legislation of its opponents in the belief that, when it can obtain power, its will, in turn, is sure of translation into statute. Both parties, doubtless, must so act as not to outrage the sentiments of any considerable part of the electorate and so prick it into insurgency. But, granted normal wisdom in a Government, the thesis of Parliamentary government is that the party which can command a majority in the House of Commons is entitled to govern in terms of its will."[1]

[1] *The Crisis and the Constitution*, p. 45.

The soundness of this thesis depends upon acceptance of the qualification. Governments may not display "normal wisdom." A determination to embark upon a "revolutionary policy" on the lines approved by Professor Laski would not indicate "normal wisdom" in a Government. It would certainly "outrage the sentiments of a considerable part of the electorate," and Professor Laski himself is strongly inclined to agree. In his view "the possessing classes" would probably fight rather than acquiesce. Indeed, he does not think that parliamentary government can function in the circumstances assumed. "Prudence," he asserts, "is a primary virtue in political behaviour," and he insists that what a Socialist Government does

> "must seem to be just to the bulk of opinion in society; and what it does must be done in such a way that the transition is not marked by the kind of abruptness which moves those affected to justifiable despair and indignation."[1]

That appears to rule out the policy he advocates, but doubts arise when he proceeds: "It must not sacrifice its essential principles," and, remember, "men now interpret so differently the ends that politics must serve that the victory of one set of principles is to its opponents in the nature of a catastrophe." Eventually, he arrives at the position that it is the duty of the minority to accept the consequences of defeat. That they will do so appears

[1] "A Socialist Government, unless it desires deliberately to provoke revolution, cannot ride rough-shod over the vested interests it proposes to attack. . . . It has to discuss, negotiate, conciliate, that it may attain the maximum possible agreement to its plans; for solutions made by consent are usually better than those which are imposed."—*Democracy in Crisis*, p. 105.

to him extremely unlikely, but he bases his contention on the ground that otherwise the position would be that "no alterations in a property system can be made save as the owners consent to it." Here, perhaps, we may find the explanation of Professor Laski's attitude. He denies or fails to recognise the possibility of progress by stages. In his view, there can be no compromise at any point in time between his rival sets of principles: it is all or nothing. To that aspect of the subject we must return later.

With regard to the exercise of majority powers, the position surely is that while the majority may be entitled to govern in terms of its will, and while it is the duty of the minority peacefully to acquiesce, the will of the majority must be directed to ends which do not place too great a strain upon the minority, and which are compatible with the maintenance of that degree of continuity requisite for the functioning of parliamentary government.[1] A party is entitled to "experiment as a government to the limits it deems reasonable of the mandate with which it is entrusted," and, if necessary, "to defend its programme with all the resources of the State behind it," but its programme must be adapted to the conditions of parliamentary democracy. It must not seek a mandate for a "revolutionary policy." The primary virtue of prudence is necessary not only in the application of policies but

---

[1] Mr. J. Middleton Murry, who advocates an abrogation of the two-party system "and all that that abrogation implies," and desires a "British form of 'the revolutionary dictatorship of the proletariat'," rightly urges as against the Labour Party that "the essential of the two-party system" is "that the party in power will enact no fundamental legislation which cannot be retained by the party in opposition when it achieves power."—*The Adelphi*, April, 1934, p. 6.

P

also in their formulation. Moreover, "mandates" need interpretation in the light of the varying motives from which they are accorded, and in the light of changing circumstances. Regard must also be paid to the position of the minority, and the practical application of policies modified accordingly.

6. *Alleged Defects in the Political System*

The assumption that a "revolutionary policy" is not inconsistent with parliamentary methods is strengthened by the contention that certain defects in the constitution are exploited, and extra-parliamentary methods of obstruction and "sabotage" employed, by Labour's opponents. The view is that were it not for these things, a revolutionary policy could be carried out by parliamentary methods. At the same time, the contention that Labour's opponents are unlikely to abandon their nefarious practices is used to justify departure from the customary parliamentary methods. There are several points in the argument.

First, there is the position of the House of Lords, which need not detain us long at this stage. That, as at present constituted, and with the powers remaining to it under the Parliament Act of 1911, it provides a check upon progressive governments not operative in the case of conservative governments, is obvious. The House of Lords presents the clearest possible illustration of that "weighting of the scales" of which the Labour Party so often complains. Nevertheless, the House of Lords is not in a position to defy the clearly-expressed intentions of the majority of the electorate. It is only when there are legitimate or plausible grounds for doubt as to those intentions that the House of Lords can hope successfully to resist the decisions of the House of Commons. Under the existing constitutional position, it has powers of delay only. They may be abused; on the other hand, they may be legitimately and usefully exercised, for the powers of a majority in the House of Commons may also be abused. At the same time, the powers of the House of Lords may still be excessive, and its composition is admittedly defective. We need not discuss whether or not a Second Chamber of any kind is needed. What is clear is that the announcement of an intention to embark upon a revolutionary policy by "constitutional methods" would only strengthen the case for a Second Chamber armed with effective powers. In such circumstances, many who, previously, might have regarded with equanimity proposals for dispensing with a Second Chamber, may well take a very different line. Clearly, the House of Lords would be justified on democratic grounds in rejecting the Socialist League's proposed "Emergency Powers Bill."

The monarchy is another institution which has not escaped criticism as a potential instrument in the hands of Labour's opponents. The constitutional rectitude and neutrality as between parties displayed by our monarchs since Queen Victoria's accession, especially during the last thirty years, seems to provide little scope for adverse criticism of their actions. However, Professor Laski, for one, has achieved the difficult task. The National Government of 1931, he contends, was "born of a Palace Revolution." [1] Mr. MacDonald was the "King's nominee," and is the

[1] *The Crisis and the Constitution*, p. 34.

"King's favourite": he is compared with Lord Bute in 1760, and also, quaintly enough, with Fox in 1782. This interpretation of the crisis of 1931 would hardly deserve serious consideration were it not for the degree of popularity which it has achieved. The National Government is characterized as "a union of opposites to oust a third rival from power," in which the King was the determining factor. The third rival, apparently, was Mr. Henderson (unless, perhaps, it was Mr. Lloyd George!), and one of Professor Laski's main grievances is that the King did not consult Mr. Henderson or any of his Labour colleagues. If, however, there is one thing about the crisis of 1931 more certain than that Mr. Henderson could not have formed an administration capable of dealing with the situation, it is that he would have declined to attempt it. That the King played an important part in the formation of the National Government is plain enough; that he acted from anti-Labour motives or with an anti-Labour bias is a suggestion for which not the slightest shred of evidence is presented. Whenever there is a confused party situation, whenever there are more than two parties, or even when one of the two parties is divided, however temporarily, then the personal, as distinct from the formal, powers of the monarch come into play. In so far as the King was instrumental in bringing about the formation of the National Government, he was carrying out an important and necessary part of his duties. Assuming, as was the case, that the Government could not continue in office, and had empowered the Prime Minister to resign;[1] and assum-

---

[1] My authority for this statement is Lord Passfield, *The Political Quarterly*, January–March, 1932, p. 8.

ing, as was also the case, that a dissolution was undesirable; then it was the King's duty to take the necessary steps to form a new Government. On the legitimate assumption that a Government composed exclusively of members of another party was impracticable, the King, in such circumstances, had somehow to bring individuals into a combination that would secure majority support in the House of Commons, and ensure that government was carried on. The particular combination achieved was not, naturally enough, generally approved, but had it not been formed, some other combination would have to have been secured, or an admittedly undesirable dissolution resolved upon. It is, in fact, difficult to see what practicable alternative there was to the Government constituted. Parties and groups would have been aligned in essentially the same way. Professor Laski evidently regards Mr. MacDonald's continued Premiership as the intolerable thing, explicable only by reason of the King's personal favour. He objects that Mr. MacDonald was not a party leader, but only a very eminent private Member. That is not strictly the case, either in form or in fact, but, assuming it were, Professor Laski must be well aware, from continental as well as from British experience, that a Cabinet drawn from several parties or groups is often headed by "a very eminent private Member."

Setting the past aside, however, the position of the monarchy is seriously affected by the proposal to pursue and apply "a revolutionary policy"; not, as is suggested, because the monarch is bound to disapprove of the aims of the party attempting such a policy, but because the attempt is certain to lead to a grave

political crisis in which it will be extremely difficult
for the monarch to avoid the appearance of departing
from his neutral supra-party position. Parliamentary
government itself would be endangered, and the King
has personal duties and responsibilities to the community. We have seen that the advocates of the
Socialist "Plan" announce their intention to demand
in advance of assuming office guarantees from the
monarch that he will use his prerogative to overcome
any opposition by the House of Lords to their proposed
Emergency Powers Act. The King would be entitled
on strictly constitutional, and on broad democratic
grounds, to refuse that demand.[1] The demand itself
would be unprecedented; so would the declared motives
behind it. The need for the so-called "emergency
powers," real or assumed, would arise solely from the
nature of the policy proposed to be followed. The
King is not bound in any way to facilitate the passage
of such legislation, especially in view of the consequences likely to result from its application. To make
acceptance of office conditional upon his concession

[1] The constitutional position was stated by the late Lord Oxford
(then Mr. Asquith) in the House of Commons on February 21st,
1910:—

"I tell the House quite frankly that I have received no such
guarantee, and that I have asked for no such guarantee. In my
judgment it is the duty of responsible politicians in this country,
as long as possible and as far as possible, to keep the name of the
Sovereign and the prerogatives of the Crown outside the domain
of party politics. If the occasion should arise, I should not hesitate
to tender such advice to the Crown as in the circumstances the
exigencies of the situation appear to warrant in the public interest.
But to ask, in advance, for a blank authority, for an indefinite
exercise of the Royal Prerogative, in regard to a measure which
has never been submitted to, or approved by, the House of Commons,
is a request which, in my judgment, no constitutional statesman
can properly make, and it is a concession which the Sovereign
cannot be expected to grant."—Quoted in *The Life of Lord Oxford
and Asquith*, Vol. I, p. 273.

of the guarantees demanded would be to place him in a gravely invidious position. Whatever his decision might be, it would be construed by one side or the other as an abandonment of his neutrality. Indeed, it is announced in advance that "any decision on the King's part which looks towards delay in the consummation of a Socialist policy" would "necessarily" be so regarded.[1]

The monarch is "a contingent source of independent authority in the State." In any time of crisis (even if it is only a ministerial crisis), that independent authority may have to be exercised. A demand for the guarantees specified, if made an issue at the preceding General Election, would be sufficient in all probability to secure the defeat of the party presenting it. But, assuming that were not the outcome, its approval by a majority of the electorate would still not be sufficient ground for the King's concession of it. If a party enjoying majority support forgets its duty to the community as a whole, the monarch is not obliged to follow suit. The circumstances envisaged would be those of a grave political crisis. As a source of independent authority, the monarch would be free to act in what he conceived to be the best interests of the community; indeed, it would be his duty so to act. There has been much hypothetical argument about what would follow a refusal of the guarantees. One point arising merits attention. The consequent refusal of the Socialist Party to take office, and the formation of a minority administration, followed by a dissolution, might result in victory for the new government. That, it must be admitted, is more than possible.

[1] Laski, *The Labour Party and the Constitution*, p. 26.

In that event, would not the monarch's action be clearly vindicated on democratic grounds? Would it be justifiable to assert that his prerogative had been exploited by Labour's opponents, or that he had departed from his non-partisan attitude? Undoubtedly, the charges would be made, and believed by many. It would be impossible to keep the Sovereign's name out of the electoral contest: but the responsibility for that, surely, would rest upon those who placed him in the predicament of having to exercise his independent authority.

It is not, however, merely a question of demanding guarantees for the creation of peers to overcome the opposition of the House of Lords to the proposed Emergency Powers Act, and to secure the abolition of that assembly. The claims presented involve the abolition of the monarch's "contingent independent authority." He is to be confined to the functions of advice, encouragement and warning which are his only political functions of importance when parliamentary government is working normally. In other words, he is to become an agent of a policy involving the destruction of parliamentary government. The safeguard which his contingent independent authority provides for democracy is to be eliminated. That, of course, is a corollary of the "Plan." The Socialist "planners" are to insist, as a condition of taking office, on "the automatic right to a dissolution of parliament whenever this is considered by its leaders to be desirable." Further, the monarch's remaining personal prerogatives are to go. The right to refuse assent to legislation, the right to exercise a personal discretion in the choice of a Prime Minister, the right to dismiss a ministry, and, presumably, the right to dissolve Parliament, are all to be eliminated. These powers, of course, are of importance only when parliamentary government is not functioning smoothly; but they are none the less of great contingent value to democracy, as, once again, Australian experience shows.[1]

The conclusion to be drawn from all this is that the neutrality of the Crown is assured so long as the conditions of parliamentary government are adhered to. The Labour Party has had no cause for complaint on this score, and, to do it justice, has made none as a Party. If it should be responsible for a departure from the principles of parliamentary government, it has no right to count on the acquiescence of the monarch, just as it has no right to count on the acquiescence of its opponents.

[1] "If the acknowledged responsibility of Ministers to the country limits the representative authority of the elected Chamber and justifies an appeal by Ministers to the country from that Chamber, that responsibility cannot be considered in terms only of a right of Ministers to consult the electors; it involves the right of the electorate to be consulted. The New South Wales case illustrates some at least of the circumstances that may arise from the intransigeance of Party, or the introduction of responsibility to extra-constitutional organs in supersession of Parliament and the electorate alike. Other circumstances may be imagined without difficulty, or may be supplied as investigation discloses the operations of the Lang Ministry and the conditions surrounding it. The Crown is the custodian of this right of the electorate. That the dismissal of a Ministry and the consequent dissolution might bring the Crown into the arena of Party conflict is true; and that in itself is a reasonable assurance that the power would not be exercised save in the gravest circumstances. But even if that risk were greater than it is, so long as the Crown makes no higher claim than to be assured that its ministry is not imposing itself upon an electorate whose support it has lost, or which it repudiates, it would not affect the duty or the responsibility of the Crown. For the Crown is not an end in itself; like every other institution of government, it exists for the sake of the country."—Sir Harrison Moore, *The Quarterly Review.*

Apart from the Monarchy and the House of Lords, there are other factors which, it is alleged, weight the scales against the Labour Party. From this standpoint, a strong case may be presented, for example, against the remaining elements of plural voting in our electoral system; and for restricting the use of motor vehicles by party organisations at elections, and providing such facilities as may be needed on a non-party basis. Nothing, perhaps, arouses greater resentment in the minds of Labour partisans than the undoubted advantage which the extensive and unregulated use of motor vehicles usually gives to their opponents. This, of course, is only one aspect of a wider criticism of all indirect advantages resulting from the possession of greater financial resources. Such advantages are often greatly exaggerated, for the influence of wealth upon the formation of political opinion is only one of many factors in the situation, and can be effectually countered. Moreover, it is difficult to see how such influences can be eliminated, and the important point in this connection is that they certainly cannot be removed by a departure from democratic methods.

Labour people often complain bitterly of misrepresentation in the great popular newspapers. The nature of the influence exercised upon public opinion by the Press combines is, however, deplored by all intelligent democrats, irrespective of party. That influence, again, is often over-estimated; nor is it exerted exclusively against Labour.[1] Moreover, the

---

[1] It is interesting to note that at the moment two of the four great London morning newspapers are supporting the Labour Party, while all four, together with the three evening newspapers, are bitterly antagonistic to the Government.

problem presents obvious difficulties. Powers of regulation exercisable by governments might result in restriction of free discussion, unless carefully delimited and safeguarded against abuse. The general aim of any proposed legislation should be extension of the sphere of discussion rather than suppression, and something might be done on such lines. In view of the mischievous effects of false and irresponsible reports and rumours, particularly in international politics, the Government should have the power to compel publication of official denials and corrections in such a way as to secure adequate publicity. Whether or not this method could be extended to protect others from the effects of falsehood and misrepresentation is a question which merits serious consideration.

On the general issue of misrepresentation, of course, no person who judges the matter with any degree of impartiality can accept the contention that the Labour Party alone suffers from that regrettable habit.

7. *"Sabotage" by Labour's Opponents*

More important, however, in Labour minds is the possibility of what is often called "sabotage" of an extra-parliamentary nature. It is now a commonplace of propaganda in certain circles that "capitalist interests," or, more particularly, "financial interests," seek to nullify the policy of a Labour Government and to render its position untenable. It is alleged that they have done so in the past, and asserted that they will attempt to do so again in the future. It is this belief which largely accounts for the feeling that parliamentary methods cannot be relied upon, and at the same time provides the excuse and popular justification for proposals to exercise "emergency powers."

The possibility of extra-parliamentary obstruction, as distinct from definitely illegal resistance, is always present; nor, incidentally, is it confined to one side. The Trade Unions, for instance, have sometimes threatened to use their industrial power to bring pressure upon governments, and on one occasion they have actually employed that power, whether intentionally or not, for the purpose. But, faced with any actual obstruction of this kind, a Government need not depart from ordinary practices. It can ask Parliament for such powers as may be deemed necessary in order to deal with it, and, if those powers are refused, it can then appeal to the electorate.

That answer, however, does not satisfy some Labour partisans. Supposing, they say, in such circumstances, the electorate refuses to support a Labour Government; supposing that it is panic-stricken as the result of a financial crisis engineered by Labour's opponents, and bamboozled by their propaganda; is that to be tolerated? If it were, it would mean that a Labour Government could always be prevented by its opponents from carrying its policy into effect. Therefore, it must be prepared to adopt other measures. The implication of this argument is confirmed by the plans we have been considering. It is that Labour should refuse to submit to the verdict of the electorate, and should resort to methods of dictatorship. Willingness to consult the electorate is, of course, one of the acid tests of democracy.

It is urged that the advent of Labour to power will be followed by an attempt to produce a grave

financial crisis. The attempt will begin, indeed, as
soon as the announcement of a Labour victory at the
polls, for "the ruling class will go to almost any
length to defeat Parliamentary action if the issue is
the direct issue as to the continuance of their financial
and political control." Is there any justification for
these fears? In one sense there obviously is. If a
Labour victory is the declared prelude to the immediate
socialization of the Bank of England and the Joint
Stock Banks (and of much else besides), there are
bound to be disturbing financial reactions.[1] But that
does not mean that there will be an organised "flight
from the pound." No "capitalist conspiracy," or
"bankers' plot," would be needed to bring that
about. The financial crisis would be produced by
Labour's announced financial programme. The policy
of our constitutional revolutionaries is to create a crisis,
and then to take emergency powers to deal with it.

Is there any basis for the suggestion that there has
been "capitalist sabotage" in the past? No convincing evidence is as yet forthcoming. The affirmative
opinion held by many Labour people is largely the
outcome of the rashly distorted account of the crisis
of 1931 assiduously propagated by certain Labour
spokesmen and writers. Professor Laski's effort in
this connection is a typical version of the "Bankers'
Ramp" charge with which the country became
familiar in 1931, and deserves reproduction.

"As in the months before the election, so during the
election itself, capitalist interests set themselves to organising the flight from the pound in the event of a Labour

[1] Indeed, Mr. Cole argues that nothing can be done to build
Socialism without undermining capitalist confidence.

victory . . . the electorate was bluntly told . . . that it
must either return the Tories to power to preserve the
interests of property, or precipitate a financial crisis. . . .
We are informed that the electorate cannot choose a Labour
Government, with a programme like that set out for
acceptance last October (1931) except at the cost of a
grave financial crisis. . . . This is equivalent to an announcement that a Labour Government will be prevented by
financial interests from pursuing a Socialist policy if it
is returned to power. The will of the House of Commons
cannot prevail. The will of the electorate is impotent. . . .
The centre of effective authority lies in the hands of a
small knot of financiers, responsible, let it be added, to
no one, who will have the fate of the nation in their hands.
If they are dissatisfied with the plans of such a Labour
Government, they will, in effect, wreck the pound."[1]

The attitude displayed towards the electorate in
this passage is interesting. Presumably, the majority
of the electors, though anxious to support the Labour
Party's programme, thought it wise to bow before the
threats of "a small knot of financiers"! If, indeed,
the majority of electors, or a sufficient number of
them, are so liable to panic, so easily swayed by certain
kinds of propaganda, or so timid that they will give
way to threats, these are facts which, of course, must
be recognized and taken into account, if democratic
methods are accepted. They constitute difficulties
which must be overcome by such methods, and not
evaded by a departure from them. (It remains highly
questionable whether they can be so evaded.) If
electors get into a panic about Labour policy, it can
only be because they dread what they think will be the
consequences of that policy. If they are mistaken

[1] *The Crisis and the Constitution*, p. 48 et seq.

about the consequences, then the Labour Party must endeavour to put them right. If they are not mistaken, then the Labour Party must set about the task of removing their fears. If electors give way to threats, it is because they are not prepared to face what they think will happen if the threats are carried out. The Labour Party must persuade them to take the risks involved, or must demonstrate that what is threatened will not or cannot be carried out. The policy recommended for electoral panics, apparently, is to give the electors something to get into a panic about. However, Professor Laski's view of the British electorate may be merely that so commonly held by the defeated party.

Although the events of 1931 are still the subject of acute party controversy, the interpretation given of them must be rejected. The charges that capitalist interests set out deliberately to "undermine foreign confidence in our financial soundness," and were organising "a flight from the pound" in the event of a Labour victory at the General Election, are clearly untenable. The causes of the financial crisis are well established. It is true that there were "predictions of woe and disaster"; it is untrue that they were "organised" by "British finance." Obviously, the last thing desired by "British finance" was a financial crisis. In so far as the warnings given were authoritative, events fully justified them. There were other warnings, of course. Predictions of impending disaster are seldom entirely absent from political controversy. After all, they are commonplaces of the cruder kinds of party wrangling. Nor were they confined, in this case, to circles politically antagonistic to Labour.

Indeed, the gloomier prognostications came from within the ranks of the Labour Party. Not only was the British financial position unstable, but British capitalism itself was tottering to its fall. The denial of the existence of any crisis by those who at the same time proclaimed the imminent decease of "capitalism" provided a sadly-needed element of humour in the situation. But, after all, it is permissible to contend that the pursuit of a particular policy will lead to unfortunate results, or the continuance of a particular situation to disaster; and the contention may be sound.

It is also perfectly true that the electorate was told that a financial crisis would result from a Labour victory at the polls. That, again, was a perfectly legitimate contention, whether in fact sound or unsound. On the assumption, legitimate though probably incorrect, that a victorious Labour Party would have proceeded to apply its election programme, the contention was, in the judgment of many people, perfectly sound. But it clearly does not follow that this was "equivalent to an announcement that a Labour Government will be prevented from pursuing a Socialist policy if it is returned to power." To say that certain consequences will follow from a certain policy or event, in certain given conditions, is not, despite the authority of Professor Laski, the same thing as saying that the consequences will, under any circumstances, be deliberately engineered.

In this matter of "sabotage," it is necessary to distinguish between actions taken by individuals in defence of what they conceive to be their interests, and actions taken with the deliberate intention of

obstructing governmental action. The former constitute a factor which, under any circumstances, has
to be taken into consideration. Such actions may
have an obstructive effect, and measures have had to
be taken against them in the past by non-Labour
governments. But the suggestion that there has been
anything in the nature of "organised" obstruction by
capitalist or financial interests is entirely devoid of
foundation. It assumes the existence of a mythical
entity known as "British capital" or "British finance."
It assumes a degree of cohesion, organisation and
determination, in the "interests" concerned, wholly
lacking up to the present, and unlikely to be developed
save under the pressure of revolutionary attack.
Much has been made of the alleged "dictation" of
the "bankers," or, more specifically, of the Bank of
England. The relations between the latter and the
Treasury are necessarily intimate, though their precise
nature in any given situation is unascertainable by the
general public. Undoubtedly, the influence of the
Bank in financial matters is considerable. That is
inevitable and proper, for the experts have to be
consulted, and their advice necessarily carries great
weight. If the Bank were directly under State control,
its influence upon policy would remain. Its officials
would be civil servants: under existing conditions,
they enjoy a more independent status, but they are,
of course, subject to parliamentary control, like other
citizens. They act, indeed, within certain limits pre-
scribed by the legislature, and they act also in consultation with the Government. There is no ground
for the supposition that illegitimate influence has
been brought to bear upon any government, or that

Ω

any government which so desired could not override opposition by the Bank to its wishes. Nor is there any basis in the suggestion that the policy of the Bank in recent years has been deliberately opposed to the public interest. Its critics have been numerous, but they have not been confined, of course, to the Labour Party. Indeed, differences of view concerning financial policy have cut right across party divisions.

On the general issue of extra-constitutional or definitely illegal resistance, the conclusion to be drawn from our past experience is that if a government accepts the implications of the democratic method it has nothing serious to fear. The one important piece of evidence which may be cited in dissent is the behaviour of certain sections of the Unionist Party in the Ulster crisis. It is significant, however, that the one modern case of proposed forcible resistance to a government arose in connection with a dispute which was not, primarily, of an economic nature. The view that in the past the "possessing classes" have yielded only to force cannot be reconciled with the facts of British political history. It carries with it the quite untenable assumption that no serious limitations have ever been imposed upon the political privileges or the economic power of the classes "in possession" at any given time. The contention is supported, of course, by the argument that no "fundamental" concessions have been asked of them; but that point has already been dealt with. The concessions demanded have often been regarded as "fundamental" by all concerned. Professor Laski has pointed out that "the decision to repeal the Corn Laws aroused widespread indignation; but the men who resented it felt that its acceptance was preferable to the alternative of revolution." That preference has operated, of course, in other cases, and it will continue to operate; but it must not be presumed upon.

"All social change is an interference with the vested interests of some definite time. About these there have accreted sentiments, emotions, ideas, which make their possessors fearful of the results of challenge to them. Successful change, therefore, is for the most part change which does not so outrage the men who protect those interests as to make them prefer conflict to the surrender of the things that change involves."[1]

The point could not have been better put. Men must not be asked to surrender too much all at once. That is the condition which those with revolutionary aims have to bear in mind.

8. *"The Impossibility of Gradualism"*

Why then do some of those who recognise this limitation continue to advocate "immediate, far-reaching and simultaneous changes affecting the entire social system"? Here we encounter another popular argument. "Gradualism," so far from being inevitable, is held to be impracticable. It is difficult to discover any rational basis for this view. Its exponents rely, for the most part, on glib phrases and dogmatic assertions. At times the very possibility of stages seems to be denied, or unrecognised. "There can be no compromise"; "there is no half-way house";

[1] Laski, *Democracy in Crisis*, p. 216.

"we must demolish the old building before starting the new." The general tone of this propaganda, with its denunciations of "gradualism," and its talk of "destroying the capitalist system," fosters the impression. Much of it, of course, is mere rhetoric. Nevertheless, it is insisted that "gradualism" cannot work, though what is meant by "gradualism" it is not always easy to discover. Mr. Cole defines it as "a slow infusion of Socialistic mechanisms and policies into the existing economic order. Socialism is thus to arise out of Capitalism by a gradual, unabrupt, and painless transition; and nothing must be done in its making to hinder, in the meantime, the smooth and successful working of the system which it is to supplant." This policy is declared to be impossible. "The result is almost complete paralysis." It is, in the popular phrase, "bolstering up the capitalist system."

It is necessary to enquire how far Mr. Cole's own policies differ from those of the "gradualists." In his case, the transition is to be rapid and abrupt, but it is to be gradual. Mr. Cole tells us that Socialism cannot be introduced all at once. It is not pretended that "a complete system of Socialism" can be instituted "at a single blow." Moreover, he mentions a number of possible circumstances (including, significantly, the extent and nature of a Socialist Government's majority), in which the plans will have to be modified. He feels obliged, indeed, to defend his policy against a possible charge that it is only a re-statement of the "moderate" position. He insists that it is not a "gradualist programme." Of course, he is right in contending that it differs vitally from what he calls "the older policies of 'gradualism,'" but as that

implies, it is "gradualist" in one sense of the term
at any rate. Mr. Cole and his friends are going to
proceed by stages, but by big and rapid stages.
Furthermore, he also wants the transition to be
as painless as possible. He hopes it will be orderly,
and he is most anxious to avoid an interval of
economic and social chaos. Somehow, therefore,
our economic and social life is to continue to
function "smoothly and successfully." This, presumably, in his case, would not be "making Capitalism
successful"; it would not be "bolstering up the
capitalist system." Since he wishes to avoid even a
temporary breakdown, he would support, presumably,
at any stage, measures designed to prevent such a
breakdown; and in such an event, there could be no
suggestion, of course, of "abandonment of Socialism"
or of "treachery" to the cause.

Yet Mr. Cole contends that "the conception of a
'moderate' Labour Party, working at once to make
Capitalism successful and to dose it with very
small instalments of Socialism, will not work."
Leaving out of account the implied identification
of "capitalism" with "the existing economic and
social order," we are given to understand that
very large instalments of Socialism *are* practicable.
How large must the instalments be before they
become practicable? The answer given is that
"the key positions of capitalist society" must be
transferred immediately to Socialist control. Apparently, there can be no divided control of the "key
positions." It is quite possible for a partially capitalist
society to function smoothly and successfully provided
"the key positions" (whatever they may be) are under

Socialist control; but it is quite impossible for it to function if such positions remain under capitalist control. We are not given any explanation of this paradox. If it were presented in terms of possible sabotage or resistance, or mere "undermining of capitalist confidence," it would obviously be unconvincing, since, under the conditions assumed, such possibilities become probabilities. There are, of course, difficult problems of co-ordination involved in any transitional period, but there is no reason to suppose that these are greater in the one case than in the other. The apparently slower method is, in this respect, at least as practicable as the apparently speedier one.

Mr. Cole, as a matter of fact, concedes its technical (and even its political) practicability. He asserts that "the logic of events will force even Conservatives to adopt many measures of partial socialisation." Indeed, he admits that they have already done much in this direction; but, he says, "if this is all that needs doing, there is no need for a Labour Party at all." That statement explodes the myth of the "impossibility of gradualness." It also indicates a failure to recognize the parts played by the respective parties in the achievement of any political ends under democratic conditions. It has been seen that, under those conditions, both parties (or all parties) make their contributions. Socialism, if and in so far as it is achieved, will be achieved as a result of the reciprocal activity of the parties. To say that because the Conservative Party makes and will make a contribution to the desired end, there is no need for a Labour Party at all, implies non-recognition of this reciprocal activity.

The fact is that the Conservative Party would not make that contribution, or would not go so far in making it, were it not for the existence of the Labour Party and the pressure it exerts.

Mr. Cole's policy differs essentially from the older policies of gradualism because it is incompatible with the retention of parliamentary democracy. It cannot be carried out on the democratic basis of voluntary general agreement or acquiescence. It is therefore far less practicable in reality than the older policies of gradualism. The argument that the latter have been proved impossible by experience is feeble in the extreme. It is based upon the two Labour Governments of 1924 and 1929–31, which provide a most inadequate test. Nothing, it is said, could be done by those Governments to build Socialism, proceeding as they were on the lines of the traditional "gradualist" policy. It has to be granted, of course, that they were minority governments, and that the majority of their supporters were anything but convinced Socialists. Resort has to be made, therefore, to the fact that they did not decide to stand or fall on a "really socialist issue," a point which is entirely irrelevant.

There is a further argument of some importance. It is contended that the older policies of "gradualism" are *no longer* practicable because of the changed economic situation. Capitalism, it is said, is no longer a progressive or stable system. Therefore, those from whom concessions will be asked will be less able, and less willing, to make them.[1] If the point is sound,

[1] The argument is confused by the introduction of the question of the extent to which social services can be extended by means of higher taxation. But this matter of "squeezing the capitalist

then, clearly, the demand for much more drastic concessions is most unlikely to meet with a willing response. But, surely, if "capitalism" is faced with difficulties which it cannot surmount, then there will be a greater readiness to consider socialist proposals, and the effect of demands for immediate revolutionary change will be to alienate support which might otherwise be forthcoming. However, the belief that "capitalism" is doomed to decline is based on a dangerously short-run view characteristic of every period of economic depression. Consideration of it would take us beyond the scope of this book, but it is by no means impossible that what is called "capitalism" will recover from this depression as from so many others, that the main problems common to such crises will be solved, and that "capitalism" will go on from strength to strength. Granted that the economic difficulties of the time involve pressure upon the workers' standard of life, the connected view that these must result in a demand for "fundamental" change is unwarranted by the facts. The associated contention that people will not tolerate any reduction in their standards is equally unwarranted. The alternative threatens them with more serious reductions still, and worse besides.

Those who advocate "revolutionary" policies do not do so because "moderate" policies are impracticable, but simply because the latter are unacceptable to them. No change of circumstances which has taken

orange" is also irrelevant. It cuts right across the division of opinion we are examining. That there are limits to the process has been urged most strongly by supporters of the "gradualist" school in the Labour Party; and refusal to recognize those limits was characteristic of the majority of the "revolutionary" school.

place affects the essentials of the position so far as political methods are concerned. "Gradualness," in the literal sense, there must always be. No statesmen, not even revolutionary dictators, can achieve their ends at will. It is one thing to make a law : another to apply it. To issue a decree is simple : to give practical effect to it may be extremely difficult. Even then, the actual results may not conform to expectations. Unforeseen obstacles may be disclosed, and unforeseen distractions may arise. Even dictators cannot attempt at once all they may wish to attempt. The use of violence may occasionally lead to a rapid conquest of political power, but that it has not the same efficacy in changing social conditions has been clearly demonstrated by Bolshevik experience. It is worthy of note that Hitler's brief tenure of power has already turned him into an avowed "gradualist."[1] However, if democratic parliamentary methods are to be adhered to, then the gradualness that excludes revolutionary policies (i.e. policies intended to produce abrupt and far-reaching changes in the ways of living to which large numbers of people are accustomed), is, always has been, and always will be, inevitable. The statement of this fact made by Mr. Sidney Webb (Lord Passfield) remains to-day in all respects as accurate as when it was presented to the Labour Party Conference in 1923.

[1] "The Nazi revolution is closed. This revolution, as a revolution, has achieved everything which it could be hoped to accomplish. . . . A revolution can never accomplish a programme by itself. It can only clear a way for forces which have adopted a definite policy, and are in a position to guarantee that it is to be carried out. Revolutions merely effect an overthrow of established power. Only evolution can alter conditions."—Proclamation to the Nazi Party Rally, Nuremberg, September 5th, 1934.

9. *The Limitations of Parliamentary Methods*

No one can lay down in advance what precisely can or can not be achieved by parliamentary methods. That which is impracticable in one set of circumstances may not be so in another.[1] "Circumstances must come in, and are to be made a part of the Matter of which we are to judge." The "inevitability of gradualness," we repeat, does not rule out the possibility of rapid change.[2] Popular opinion is not, of course, always averse from change. It is not averse from experiment, although a great deal depends, naturally enough, upon the persons who propose to experiment: confidence in them is requisite. State ownership and control of the Bank of England, for example, might well be accepted at the hands of Mr. Neville Chamberlain or Mr. Herbert Morrison and rejected at the hands of Mr. Cole or Sir Oswald Mosley. The methods of approach are all-important. A proposal heralded as an attack upon the citadel of capitalism is

[1] This may be true of policies which are labelled "revolutionary," a term which is often used very loosely. It is one thing to present a policy involving a rapid and radical change in the ways in which people live, and another to propose concrete schemes for dealing with particular problems. A new monetary policy may be devised which may be termed "revolutionary," and which would, if applied, exercise far-reaching effects upon economic life, but it might not be revolutionary in the sense of compelling people suddenly to change their ways of living. Similarly the "revolutionary" nature of proposals for extending national ownership and control depends largely upon the proposed conditions of transference.

[2] The only rational ground for criticism from a Socialist standpoint of the actions of the minority Labour Governments, would be that, in the circumstances, more might have been attempted and achieved. If criticism had been kept within those limits, then it would hardly concern us here, although it may be suggested that the members of the Government are themselves likely to be the best judges of all the circumstances. That, however, has not been the case. The whole policy based upon "the inevitability of gradualness" has been called in question.

less likely to attract support than the same proposal
advocated on limited practical grounds.

The restrictions upon action imposed by democratic
conditions should not be over-stressed. They do not,
of course, mean that parties and governments must be
content to find out what "the people" want and then
to propose it. It is their business to mould "public
opinion"; to give a lead. It is not even necessary
to obtain prior consent for all actions taken by governments; indeed, that is not possible. The "mandates"
given are general; they do not cover the whole ground;
and they need interpretation. There is wide scope,
as we have noted, for discretionary action. Measures
which might not have obtained previous sanction
are frequently found acceptable after they have been
taken. There is a margin within which governments
can act in advance of "public opinion."

Political programmes, however, should be based
upon a close knowledge of the views and interests
of the members of the community, and of the trends
of opinion. Parties should limit them at any given
time to what is practicable, and consistent with the
maintenance of parliamentary democracy. A distinction has to be drawn between the general principles
and aims of a party, and its practical programme.
Mr. Sidney Webb, in the speech above referred to,
suggested that critics of the Labour Party were
confused by this distinction. There is much truth in
that; and it would also be true to say that the members
of that Party, for the most part, have never appreciated
any such distinction. A political party seeking governmental powers cannot be a mere organisation for the
propagation of ideals and ideas (Socialist or any other).

Still less can it act in office as though it were, for instance, a body of Socialist zealots directing the affairs of an ideal Socialist community. Failure to grasp these elementary facts is an important element in the disillusionment which followed the Labour Party's advent to office. It was not that leaders omitted to point them out. It was partly because the advice and warnings of leaders were consistently scorned by influential propagandists, many of whom never accepted parliamentary methods, however much lip-service they might render to them from time to time; and partly because of the Party's lack of governmental experience. Mr. Sidney Webb, in 1923, reminded the Party that it was offering itself to the electors as an alternative government, prepared to take over the whole administration of the nation, and that it must rise to its responsibilities.

"We have, from now onward, to work and speak and act, under the sense of the liability, at any moment, to be charged with putting our plans and projects into operation." This meant "that we should not lightly commit ourselves as a party—and we should not even seek to commit the party as a party—to new or additional projects or to the details of reforms, if these belong more appropriately to a stage of greater freedom and less responsibility."

Passing judgment on the situation after the crisis of 1931, the same gentleman expressed the view that the Labour Party was "prematurely born into governmental life."

"Most of its parliamentary representatives have found it difficult, in their inexperience, to rid themselves of the mental habits of a life-long opposition to the powers that be, whilst some of them have seemed almost to regret the chance that has put them, for a time, among those powers."

What is true of many Labour parliamentarians is even more generally true of the active rank-and-file of the Party. For years they have indulged in the luxury of indiscriminate denunciation of existing society and all its works. Those who have exercised some discrimination have judged governments and policies by the standards (very vague and very general) of their Socialist ideals. For the most part, the rank-and-file, and the party propagandists, have let their moral indignation run riot. They have not realized what was involved in the formation of a political party claiming governmental powers; and, still less, what was involved in actually assuming the responsibilities of government. The fact that the Party took office on both occasions under minority conditions only emphasizes the truth of these contentions. As a whole, the Party was unwilling to face the facts of the political situation either in 1924 or in 1929–31. It was thoroughly uncomfortable. From the moment the first Labour Government took office, a cry went up that they should abandon it. That was the case also, very soon, with the second Labour Government, and considerable numbers of Labour people seem to have been relieved rather than distressed when the Labour Government resigned. They could not stand the strain of governmental responsibility, and the reason was that they had not understood the essential conditions of governmental action under parliamentary democracy, whether as a majority or as a minority party.

10. *The "Minority Government" Controversy*

The controversy in the Labour Party about minority government has been most illuminating to the student of politics. The immediate reaction to experience of government was simple: "No more minority government." Minority government was the root of the trouble; it was that which led the Party into the fatal paths of compromise, and undermined the morale of the faithful. Take office only as a majority (or, which amounts to the same thing, take office as a minority only in order "to act like a majority government," i.e. to ride for an immediate fall), and then the Party could apply its policies without let or hindrance, and preserve its principles in all their purity. This attitude still persists. Attempts to commit the Party to the policy of refusing to take office as a minority under any circumstances have been circumvented by the Party leaders, but there is no doubt that the predominant feeling in the Party is opposed to the assumption of office as a minority except for the purpose of staging a further General Election.[1] That feeling may be too powerful for the leaders on the next occasion, and, if so, the resulting situation may present dangerous features. A parliamentary deadlock offers one of the most favourable opportunities for the development of Fascism likely to arise in this country.

---

[1] The Labour Party is still bound, apparently, by the following resolution passed at the Leicester Annual Conference in 1932:— "That on assuming office, *with or without power*, definite Socialist legislation must be immediately promulgated, and that the party shall stand or fall in the House of Commons on the principles in which it has faith." The leaders may intend to ignore this resolution, but there will be some who will not allow it to be forgotten.

This simple reaction has been supplemented in certain quarters. The fact that the difference between a minority and a majority government is only one of degree is partially recognized. A Labour Party majority, it is realized, may not be a Socialist majority. At any rate, it may not be a majority of Socialists determined to "carry out fundamental measures." Therefore, such a majority must be created, if possible, before Labour again takes office. The difficulty of the task is granted. Supposing the Party obtains a majority which is not 100 per cent "genuine" (i.e. revolutionary) Socialist! That may happen, for Governments, unfortunately, are always so unpopular.

"The danger is that the present Government . . . constitutes a very large target for attack. . . . Disillusionment may produce a situation sooner than may be wished, in which the Labour Party is again confronted with the acceptance of office. We can only hope that such a situation will not arise in the near future. But if it does and their majority is inadequate, let them come in and be beaten in the first few months of their existence on a clear Socialist issue."[1]

Even with a majority, therefore, the Labour Party may, in certain circumstances refuse, in effect, to take office. Clearly, it is impossible—however long the wait may be—to jump from the position of a select minority to that of a full-blooded majority. The inevitably composite nature of a party is not yet accepted, any more than the limitations imposed upon the actions of a majority, even if it is of the full-blooded variety. In any event, it is urged, the revolutionary policy must be frankly presented to the

[1] Lord Ponsonby, *The Political Quarterly*, January–March, 1932.

electorate, so that voters have no excuse for not knowing what they are voting for. The proposed frankness is, of course, admirable, although it is evidently not so regarded by other sections of the Party. The important point, however, is that the notion of a political party refusing to take office, or taking office only for the purpose of making demonstrations, unless and until it has, not only a majority, but a majority of uncompromising zealots behind it, is one entirely divorced from the realities of parliamentary government.

The strategy of assuming office as a minority in order to strengthen the prospects of acquiring a majority at another General Election is regarded with much favour in more moderate circles. It is not, of course, a new conception in British politics, and was a factor in the decisions which led to the formation of the two Labour minority governments. Now, however, it is advocated in a different form. The idea is that, having taken office under minority conditions, a Labour Government should proceed to act as it would have acted if it had enjoyed majority support.[1] In the highly probable event of an almost immediate defeat on a vote of no confidence, the Government would at once appeal to the country.[2] It is argued

[1] The strange argument is sometimes presented that, since a Party has contested a General Election on a particular programme, it has a duty to the electorate to attempt to carry out that programme, not modified in any way, in the event of it taking office as a minority government. Whatever other grounds may be advanced in favour of such a course, it is obvious that, in such circumstances, the majority of the electorate has expressed the view that it does not want that unmodified programme.

[2] This procedure is based on the unsound assumption that the Government's advice in favour of a dissolution of Parliament is bound to be accepted.

that such an appeal would meet with a great response from the electorate: in all probability, Labour would obtain a majority, and the Government would be able to proceed with its programme. Such a result, though possible, would be extremely uncertain. The outcome might be a loss of support, and a consequent loss of the original opportunity to co-operate effectively with some other party or group. Supposing, however, as might well happen, the party position remained virtually unchanged. Would the Labour Government then repeat the same tactics, and stage yet another General Election, with less chance of success? Would it accept the electoral verdict, and endeavour to function as a minority government on a modified programme, in circumstances which would be less favourable than those originally obtaining? Or would it resign and go into opposition? These questions indicate that, whatever there is to be said in support of the strategy proposed, it leaves the issue of minority government unsolved, and constitutes an attempt to evade the underlying problems of co-operation and compromise. Moreover, by prolonging the parliamentary deadlock it may foster anti-parliamentary movements.

A party which is afraid of compromise, which is not prepared to undertake or share in the responsibilities of government save on terms which enable it to impose its will dictatorially upon the rest of the community, either dooms itself to futility or brings parliamentary government to a deadlock. In this country, the first is more likely to happen than the second. Nevertheless, the British Labour Party is bound to play an important part in our politics for some time to come. If it remains

R

intransigeant, the consequences for British parliamentary government may be serious if not fatal. If it desires to avoid those consequences, it has to understand the nature and accept the limitations of the democratic method. The delusive notion of "independence" must go. The attitude of non-co-operation must go. The necessity of compromise must be accepted; and the "inevitability of gradualness" fully recognised. The party must face the facts that, under democratic conditions, there can be no abrupt revolutionary changes, and that, therefore, it must be prepared to do things which are not in strict conformity either with abstract Socialist principles or Five-Year Socialist Plans, or even with the kind of election programmes which it has hitherto presented. There must be continuity of policy, even in "fundamentals," even with "capitalism." The Labour Party may be called upon to participate in government in circumstances in which its plans and projects cannot be put into operation; but where those circumstances do not obtain, then its practical programmes must be in the nature of "partial amendments of a going concern." At all costs, the life of the community must be kept functioning as smoothly and harmoniously as possible: a breakdown must be avoided.

11. " *Destroying the Capitalist System* "

The desire, even among the revolutionaries, to escape a period of "chaos and desolation" has been noted. "Duty and prudence," says Professor R. H. Tawney, "require that necessary changes should be effected without a breakdown." If that is so, then it would be

legitimate for the Labour Party to take action merely
in order to avoid a breakdown. Moreover, if the desire
to avoid a breakdown is genuine, as is assuredly the
case, then all talk about "bolstering up the capitalist
system" ought to be abandoned. A truly revolutionary
party, of course, would welcome the prospect of an
economic collapse and political chaos. No section of
the Labour Party, "moderate" or "revolutionary,"
really desires anything of the kind. Yet it has not,
at present, apparently, made up its mind whether to
welcome or to deplore the prospect of an economic
breakdown. Its spokesmen will repeatedly and joy-
fully announce the imminent fall of "the system."
Any suggestion that "the system" may not be in
such dire straits is treated with the utmost suspicion.
Of course, much of the confusion arises from the
notion that there is nothing in common between the
existing economic and social arrangements and the
kind of economic and social order Labour people wish
ultimately to bring into being. If that were indeed
the case, if "Socialism" can only be achieved by its
substitution as a whole for "Capitalism" as a whole
(or even if "the key positions" had to be transferred
as a whole to Socialist control), then nothing could
prevent an economic breakdown. Yet references to
"supplanting" Capitalism by Socialism, and a thousand
others of the same kind, are continually made. The
phraseology of revolution, and the curious delight which
so many Labour spokesmen seem to take in dwelling
upon and exaggerating the economic frictions and
maladjustments of the present "system" and in
prophesying its rapid downfall, are misleading alike
to the Labour rank-and-file and to the general public.

It is strange that people should welcome what they really do not want, and even say they do not want.

Faced with the actual prospect of a "crash," there is little doubt that the great majority of the Labour Party would do their utmost to avert it, and would range themselves on the side of order in the event of the situation being exploited by any revolutionary movement. They would not wittingly do anything to contribute to an economic disaster, or to the worsening of the present economic situation. They might, however, do so unwittingly. The moral is plain. The practical policies of the Party, even though they may be considered economically sound, must be so designed as to rule out abrupt and far-reaching changes certain to lead to grave economic dislocation. This would hold good even if such changes were consistent with the maintenance of parliamentary government. It has been shown that they are not.

12. *The Conservative Party and the Democratic Method*

Our consideration of the attitude of the Labour Party towards parliamentary government will have conveyed a misleading impression if it has been regarded as more than illustrative of our general argument. The future of British political institutions is dependent in at least equal measure upon the policies pursued by the party or parties of the Right. Danger from that quarter may appear negligible at the moment. There is the British Union of Fascists, it is true, although it is doubtful how far Fascism can be regarded as a movement of the Right. It has dangerous potentialities, however, appealing as it does to Right as well as to Left, because the spirit of which it is an expression is no more confined to its own ranks than is Communism to the Communist Party of Great Britain. Circumstances may arise in which it may constitute a serious menace to our democratic political system.

The relations of Conservative leaders with their parties provide ample evidence of the fact that failure to appreciate the nature and implications of democratic methods is not by any means confined to the Left. Impatience with the restraints imposed by democracy is, in general, no less conspicuous on the Right than on the Left. A change in the political situation at the expense of the Right may bring that impatience to the front in this country, and transform it into a menacing political force. Obstinate resistance to change, and a determination at all costs to retain political privileges and economic advantages, constitute as serious a threat to democratic government as any "revolutionary" policy.

One searching test of continued Conservative adhesion to the democratic method has yet to come. It will be applied if and when a government is returned to power with a clear majority mandate to effect important changes of a socialistic character. The responsibilities and limitations imposed by the democratic method upon such a government have been stated. Complementary democratic duties devolve upon the Opposition in the circumstances assumed. Acquiescence in majority decisions is essential; there must be scrupulous abstention from any form of extra-constitutional obstruction or illegal resistance, even if it should be felt that the governmental majority is abusing its formal powers; and, more difficult but none the less desirable, severe restraint in utilising whatever opportunities may arise for parliamentary or other legal forms of obstruction. The Opposition must rely exclusively upon the democratic weapons of discussion, persuasion, and peaceful protest.

The suspicion that many Conservatives will adhere to the Parliamentary system only so long as it serves their purposes is a factor making for recourse to non-democratic methods. It is important, therefore, that this suspicion should be removed as far as possible, not merely by verbal declarations, but by conformity to the democratic spirit in the conduct of Conservative policy, particularly during the period before the situation envisaged arises.

The Conservative may ask what grounds exist for the suspicion. The question has been partially dealt with already, but there are three major points which require to be emphasised and elaborated. The first relates to the Ulster Crisis; the second to the position of the House of Lords; and the third to Fascism.

The conduct of prominent Unionist leaders in regard to the Ulster question, the illegal actions in which they participated or at which they connived, the incitement to and threats of armed resistance to the impending application of an Act of Parliament, the relations of important military servants of the State with the Unionist Party, have bequeathed a legacy of suspicion which the Conservative Party, if it believes in democratic methods, has a duty to do its utmost to eradicate. Notwithstanding the peculiarity of the issues raised by the Home Rule Bills (which distinguish them sharply from the issues of domestic politics); granting that the Unionist case in regard to Ulster was a strong one,

and that the behaviour of other parties to the controversy was not always defensible on democratic
grounds; and allowing for the possibility that the
actions referred to constituted a gigantic bluff; there
is no doubt that what happened gave a severe shock
to democratic government, the effects of which have
still to be taken into account.

The attitude of the House of Lords towards progressive governments in the past also gives rise to
justifiable apprehensions about the future. Here the
Conservative Party has a special responsibility. Its
influence in the House of Lords is normally decisive.
That being so, the duty is imposed upon it of seeing
that the powers of the House of Lords are used only on
clearly democratic grounds. Admittedly, that is an
extremely difficult task, for the composition of the
Upper House is so anomalous in a democratic system
that, in any event, the charge of partisanship could
hardly be avoided. But, so long as the House of
Lords remains as it is at present, the Conservative
Party cannot evade this responsibility. In existing
circumstances, other parties suffer from a disadvantage
from which the Conservative Party is immune. That
is an obvious defect in our political system from the
democratic standpoint, and a natural source of
grievance to other parties. So long as it remains, a
democratic Conservative Party must seek to minimise
its effects by imposing upon itself a Self-Denying
Ordinance. If that is asking too much, and no doubt
it is, then the question of the reform or abolition
of the Upper House has to be faced. For a reversion
by the House of Lords to the partisan tactics of
the pre-war years would be a violation of the democratic

method bound to lead to serious trouble. So also, it must be clearly stated, would a reform of the House of Lords which maintained the predominance of one political party while abolishing the "safety valve" provided by the royal prerogative to create peers. The case for a Second Chamber, from the democratic standpoint, is strong, but no such Chamber will conform to the requirements of the democratic method unless it is so constructed that no reasonable charge can be brought against it on the ground that it is designed to favour one political party at the expense of the others. A reform of the House of Lords on democratic lines is, indeed, urgently necessary, and it is to be hoped that the Conservative Party, upon whom the chief responsibility rests, will appreciate the importance of dealing with this matter in a democratic spirit, and not with the partisan objective of crippling a Labour Government.

The third point is that in any actions which may be taken against anti-democratic movements there should be no discrimination between such movements because of the nature of the ends which they may respectively seek to achieve by dictatorial methods. There must be no combination of repressive action against one brand of revolutionaries with tolerance of another brand. Few things would be more fatal to confidence in parliamentary government than for the impression to be fostered that Conservatives are more kindly disposed to Fascism than to Communism. The tendency in certain Labour circles to excuse the methods of the Communists out of sympathy with their aims is an error of judgment which Conservatives should be scrupulously careful not to imitate. As it is, there

are far too many rank-and-file Conservatives who
think that any methods may legitimately be used
against "the menace of Socialism," and who appear
to view the Fascist movement with equanimity as an
instrument which may well be employed or allowed to
function in the last resort. Those who direct the
Conservative Party must reject all manifestations of
Fascism as vigorously and decisively as the Labour
Party leaders have rejected Communism. It is to
certain groups of what is normally Conservative
opinion that Fascism appeals most effectively, and
from which it appears to be drawing the major share
of its recruits. Just as the Labour Party has been
and is the most effective democratic instrument for
checking Communism, so the Conservative Party
should be the most effective in resisting Fascism. It
bears the main burden of responsibility in this connection.

Apart from these special considerations affecting
the Conservative Party, there should be general
acceptance, irrespective of party, of the conditions
we have attempted to state, if our parliamentary
system of government is to continue to function.
Failure to conform to them in any quarter not only
constitutes a danger in itself, but provokes similar
action in other quarters. Revolutionary policies on
the Left provide a stimulus to Fascism; Fascism in
turn breeds Communism. Obstruction of democratic
processes of change promotes revolutionary processes
of change. If important social changes desired by vast
numbers of people cannot be even partially effected
by democratic methods, then, inevitably, recourse
will be had to other methods.

13. *The Difficulties of the Liberal Party*

An omission of any reference to the Liberal Party might be misconstrued. The traditions and tenets of Liberals, as well as their present political situation, make them keen supporters of democracy; yet it would be going too far to suggest that even they fully appreciate the implications of the democratic method. In no British party has the conflict of personalities played so great a part as in the Liberal Party in the post-War years, and those conflicts have contributed notably to its decline. On the other hand, the divisions in its ranks have been due in large measure to the intermediate position of the Party, the perplexities of which have been accentuated by the nature of our electoral system. We have already stressed the difficulties of any intermediate party or group, and at the moment, of course, the official Liberal Party is one only of a number of such groups. The desirability of co-operation and compromise is impressed upon a central party or group more forcibly than upon a party which has a chance of securing majority backing; yet co-operation and compromise, however desirable and even necessary, militate against the continuance of a middle party's existence. Consequently, there may be influences within such a party directed primarily to its own preservation; and that is the more likely to be the case if the party concerned, like the Liberal Party, has great traditions because of its former position as one of the two great parties in the State. In such circumstances, the democratic desire to co-operate may be thwarted by partisan interests. It is not suggested that this has happened in the case of the Liberal Party to any serious extent; and it is readily granted that the problems of co-operation and compromise confronting such a party are extremely difficult, and may be made much more so by lack of reciprocal concessions on the part of the other parties concerned. However, it is legitimate to raise the question whether the maintenance and successful working of parliamentary government would not be promoted by the disappearance of the Liberal Party. Might not Liberal co-operation be more effectively secured by the merging of Liberal elements in both the great political parties? It is clear that the existence of the Liberal Party as a separate organisation increases the possibility of parliamentary deadlock, and weakens the moderating influences within the other political parties. There is a danger also that the Liberal Party, in order to preserve its internal cohesion and its electoral strength as far as possible, may decline to co-operate or withdraw from co-operation in circumstances when collaboration may be very desirable from the democratic standpoint.

The danger is increased by reason of the fact that the Liberals are not by any means immune from the defects from which other parties suffer. As in the case of other parties, partisanship is carried too far, and, in the Liberal case, is often rendered all the more exacerbating by the spirit of self-righteousness in which it is conducted.[1] In the Liberal Party, as elsewhere, leaders are too frequently hampered by the rigidities of the rank-and-file. Adherence to party shibboleths is as pronounced, and the necessity of

[1] The great Liberal newspapers, *The Manchester Guardian* and *The News-Chronicle*, are pre-eminent in their support of democracy, and second to none in the art of partisan misrepresentation.

compromise is as inadequately appreciated, as in the Conservative or Labour Parties.[1] These defects are all the more regrettable because the Liberal Party has perhaps most to gain from strict conformity to democratic methods and most to lose by any departure from them.

14. *Fascism and Communism*

In Sir Oswald Mosley's British Union of Fascists we have the emergence of a movement which is as avowedly anti-democratic and anti-parliamentary as any political party cares to be in these days. Sir Oswald, as might be expected from a modern would-be dictator, proposes to attain power by constitutional methods, and to establish his Fascist régime by consent of the majority. His original proposals, in the days of "The New Party," for "a fundamental revision of Parliament," bear a striking resemblance to those of Sir Stafford Cripps. Indeed, the British Fascists now accuse the Socialist League of having borrowed their notions from Sir Oswald.[2] However, the Fascists scorn the half-heartedness of Sir Stafford and the other "posturing Girondins with the heads of communists and the

---

[1] The following resolution of the Barnstaple Liberal Association in regard to Dr. Leslie Burgin, M.P., a Liberal Minister in the National Government, is instructive:—

"The Liberals of the Barnstaple Division having seen an announcement that Dr. Leslie Burgin, M.P., is to speak for Sir Basil Peto, the Conservative Member for the Division, at a political meeting in the constituency, express their protest that a Member of Parliament utilising the label 'Liberal' should take such a course. The proposed action of Dr. Burgin is regarded as being inconsistent with the democratic principles of party procedure, and out of conformity with accepted political practice. Still less is it consonant with the idea of honesty in politics, or the customary well-founded courtesies of public life."

[2] *The Blackshirt*, October 14th, 1933.
Oswald Mosley, *Blackshirt Policy*, pp. 11–12.

chicken hearts of Social Democrats"; and Sir Oswald has travelled far since 1931. That his objective is dictatorship is clearly shown by his wholesale adoption of the methods of Signor Mussolini as improved by the more "constitutional" technique of Herr Hitler. His proposals for an Emergency Powers Act, for curtailing Parliamentary discussion, and for placing Fascist M.P.'s in charge of local administration, all so closely approximating to the plans of the Socialist constitutional revolutionaries, have been expanded into a proposed Act by which the constitutionally-elected Fascist majority would proceed to hand over complete power to the Fascist Government, which would then substitute the "totalitarian" and "Corporate" State for the existing system of parliamentary government. Party politics would be abolished, that is to say, all opposition parties would be suppressed, and the "neo-Cæsarism" which is alleged to be "the modern expression of a very strong and definite tendency in the history of British thought" would be triumphantly established.

A tendency may be discerned in some quarters to view Fascism in this country merely as a political party like any other, any disturbing reflections inspired by the use of the word "Fascist" being calmed by the comfortable thought that, of course, in this country Fascism will not be accompanied by any of the brutalities and tyrannical repressions which have marked its progress on the Continent. It is then easy to lapse into the frame of mind which contemplates giving the Fascists a trial, on the assumption that a Fascist Government can be displaced as peaceably and smoothly as any other. After all, it is argued, we can decide to give the Fascists their chance, and if we do not like them we can get rid of them. It would all be perfectly legal and constitutional. The Fascists assure us of that, and make it clear that the installation and continuance of their Government would depend upon our consent.

In view of this kind of attitude, it is important that the general public should fully appreciate the drastic nature of the change in political methods advocated by the British Fascists. Sir Oswald Mosley has himself repeatedly emphasised the revolutionary nature of his objective. His "revolution by constitutional means," like that of Sir Stafford Cripps, would involve the destruction of parliamentary government. Sir Oswald, however, unlike Sir Stafford, frankly desires and proposes the abolition of parliamentary government. His aims comprise a revolution in political methods as well as the achievement of a revolutionary programme. He even accepts the term "dictatorship" as applicable to the system he advocates. His dictatorship, however, would not be a dictatorship "against the will of the people." One of Sir Oswald's favourite definitions is that "Fascism is Dictatorship in the modern sense of the word, which implies government armed by the people with power to solve problems which the people are determined to overcome." [1] It would not be a tyranny. Dictatorship, in the modern sense, is only "Leadership of the people with their willing consent." The Leader, i.e. Sir Oswald, would have "absolute authority." What is called "the principle of individual responsibility" would apply throughout the system; all the officers of the Fascist

[1] *The Greater Britain*, 1934 Edition, p. 26.

State, that is to say, would be personally responsible to the Leader, either directly or mediately, and would owe him, or their immediate superiors, unquestioning obedience. It would be a system of "voluntary discipline."

The British Fascists seek to achieve power "in the first instance" by winning a parliamentary majority at a General Election, although there are not lacking hints about the possibility of having to use "other and sterner measures."[2] Having secured a majority, they would proceed to carry through their revolution. Once again it is assumed that a majority decision represents "the will of the people," and that "the people" and "the majority" are one and the same thing. The Fascist Government would be entrusted at once with absolute authority. Under the Fascist system then to be set up, the Government would depend upon "the direct will of the people directly expressed." Sir Oswald Mosley lays great stress upon this point. It is this plausible proposal for the institution of the plebiscite which dictators, past and present, have repeatedly employed in order to propitiate democratic sentiment. It is the method of Mussolini and Hitler as it was the method of the Napoleons. Its deceptiveness is easily exposed. Sir Oswald Mosley tells us that under his system "the life and policy of the government will be submitted to the country for a 'Yes' or 'No' decision by universal franchise." If the decision is negative, then the King is to appoint a fresh Government, which would in turn submit itself to a direct vote of the people. From whence, however, is the King to draw his new

[2] ibid, *The Greater Britain*, 1934 Edition, p. 189.

Ministry? Presumably, from some other political party. But would there be any other political party? The answer to that is in the negative. Sir Oswald Mosley has not yet, apparently, declared in so many words that Fascism would suppress all opposition parties; he prefers to speak of the suppression of "party warfare."[1] Anyhow, there is no doubt whatever as to his intentions. The party system is one of the two main objects of the Fascist attack; and Parliament is the other. The Fascists do not constitute just one more British political party; their party is one which would not permit the existence of any other. We know from the experience of existing Fascist States that all political activity outside the Fascist Party is sternly repressed; and this is not one of the respects in which British Fascism would differ from other branches of the "world-wide faith." Nor could the King turn for a new Ministry to Parliament. Parliament, as we have known it, is to disappear under the Fascist régime: that is a corollary of the suppression of parties. There is to be a "Parliament" of sorts, according to Sir Oswald, but it is to be "technical" and "non-political." It would be elected on an occupational basis, and would be divested of any influence on policy and of any control over the Government. The latter would be responsible only and directly to "the people," whose power would be exercised solely through a periodical plebiscite, at which the citizens would have merely the right, and that in all probability a useless one,

[1] "Therefore the nation in voting Fascism into power will deliberately enter a new civilisation in which the Government will be given power to suppress party warfare, which it will certainly exercise."—*Blackshirt Policy*, p. 73.

of saying "No." They would not have the power to indicate an alternative Government. No alternative policies would be presented to them. No rival parties would appeal for their support. There would be no effective criticism of the Fascist Government, for that, we may legitimately infer, would be banned under the comprehensive phrase "suppression of party warfare," and the same phrase would serve, as in the case of Italy and Germany, to justify Fascist control of the Press and all other agencies for making and influencing opinion.

We are quite prepared to accept Sir Oswald Mosley's contention that in this country Fascism would assume distinctive forms; but it is clear that there would be no difference in essentials, and that, in regard to the system of government itself, British Fascism follows closely the Italian model. Tyranny, despite Sir Oswald's disclaimer, is a perfectly accurate description of it. Even in regard to the barbarities which have disgraced Fascism in Germany and Italy, there are grounds for grave doubt about the distinctiveness of the British variety. The provocative use of uniforms, the organisation of a so-called Defence Force, and the methods employed by that Force, constitute a significant departure from British traditions, and illustrate once more how faithfully the British Fascists imitate their Continental examples. In this country, however, attention has been directed too exclusively to these aspects of the matter. Their dangerous potentialities are obvious. It is clearly the duty of the democratic State not to permit its functions in regard to the maintenance of order to be usurped by any private force; and, no doubt, that duty will be strictly carried

s

out now that the events at the Olympia meeting have exposed the perils of the situation. It may well be necessary also to prohibit the use of uniforms for political purposes. On the whole, however, Fascist behaviour in these respects is a liability rather than an asset to the movement. A Fascism which shed its more obviously objectionable features would be all the more dangerous to parliamentary institutions.

The root of the trouble, from the democratic standpoint, is not to be found in uniforms or in the creation of a private army, nor even in physical brutalities, but in the Fascist rejection of all the basic principles of parliamentary democracy. The former present relatively simple problems for the democratic State; they can be dealt with by governmental action. The latter, however, cannot be countered by legislation or administrative action. Energetic defensive propaganda is demanded, and for that purpose it is requisite that people should fully understand the essential principles of that which they are anxious to defend. Fascism challenges those principles in their entirety. Its real attack is directed against the democratic principles of discussion and compromise; and the attack meets with a measure of success only because the democrat is too often half-hearted in his defence of those principles. Nothing is easier, and few things more popular, than to denounce "talk" and to demand "decisive action." Sir Oswald Mosley, like Signor Mussolini and Herr Hitler, has no objection to "talk." All three are champion talkers. What they object to is that anyone else should talk, save on their instructions. In other words, they object to free discussion. Similarly, their denunciation of compromise indicates merely intolerance of differences of opinion. It is not just "decisive action" that they want. They would object strongly to any "decisive action" on the part of others. What they want is simply to have their own way, and to override all criticism and opposition.

Fascism strikes at the very root of parliamentary democracy, which is political freedom. It is not for nothing that Sir Oswald Mosley, again in dutiful imitation of his foreign prototypes, jeers at political and parliamentary liberty. And, here again, he avails himself of arguments which so-called "democrats" have placed at his disposal. Echoing Mr. Cole and others, he exclaims: "Surely nobody can imagine that the British, as a race, are free."[1] For "only economic liberty brings real freedom"; and "that economic liberty consists of things which really affect the lives of the people, such as good wages, good houses to live in, short hours of labour, after which home and leisure can be enjoyed with family and friends."[2] To Sir Oswald, political liberty is an illusion. It is humbug. What really matters is to put an end to economic chaos, and for that purpose, he argues, it is necessary to have "the power to act." Therefore, "the reign of talk" must be ended. We must not discuss how the economic chaos is to be ended. It might be concluded that any one who is entrusted with the power to act would be able to solve our economic problems. That, however, would be a mistake. In this country, it is Sir Oswald only who has been gifted with that ability, and any one who thinks that Sir Oswald's programme would intensify rather than diminish the economic

[1] *The Greater Britain*, p. 29.
[2] *Blackshirt Policy*, p. 11.

chaos would have to keep such thoughts to himself. It is true that such a person might be able to state excellent reasons for so thinking, but he would not be allowed to state them, because that would bring back "the reign of talk."

Sir Oswald and the British Fascists, again imitating the technique of Herr Hitler, have the temerity to claim from the democratic State "the right of free speech," i.e. the right to talk. Free speech has not and will not be denied to them; and if others attempt to deprive them of it the democratic State should take the necessary action. However, the assertion of a "right" to free speech by people who are not prepared, once they have acquired power, to concede that right to others, should be recognised for the brazen effrontery it is. The Fascist, like the Communist, is accorded free speech by the democratic State not as a right but as an act of grace. The Communist whines for it; the Fascist insolently demands it. The former method is the more effective with some of our sentimental democrats, but it is high time that the hypocrisy of both should be realised.

The importance of the Fascist movement, as of Communism, consists in the problems it may raise for the democratic parliamentary State. Freedom of discussion, as we have seen, is vital to democracy. The democrat cannot, without violating his own principles, suppress or attempt to suppress the advocacy of either Fascism or Communism. It is implicit in the democratic method that people should be free to question that method itself. It follows that political association for such purposes should also be tolerated. But political association for the definite purpose of overthrowing parliamentary democracy is another matter; and here the case for tolerance is not so clear.

The problem we have to consider is not that raised by actions designed to promote the destruction by violence of the parliamentary State. The question is whether we are to allow the avowed opponents of democracy to utilise the democratic machinery for the purpose of overthrowing democracy. The answer, it is suggested, must be a decisive negative.

It is generally conceded that there is nothing incompatible with democracy in the use of the legal processes and forces of the State to suppress revolutionary action. It is not so widely recognised, however, that it is also consistent with democracy to deny to the partisans of any kind of dictatorship the power of achieving their ends by taking advantage of the apparatus of democracy. The view is sometimes expressed that to deprive an anti-democratic party of representation in Parliament is a violation of the democratic method. It is even argued that if a majority of the electors freely decide in favour of a dictatorship then it would be inconsistent for democrats to resist such a dictatorship. These contentions are founded upon a complete misunderstanding of the democratic method, as our previous interpretation of that method will have shown.

Democracy can only work provided there is fairly general acceptance of it. A Parliament in which there are parties whose policy is to obstruct and, if possible, to wreck the whole system is a Parliament which cannot function properly. If such parties are numerically small, they may not in practice have any ill effects, although even a small anti-democratic party can do much mischief if parties are fairly evenly balanced. But, if such parties constitute an important element in Parliament, then it may be brought to a state of complete deadlock. It may well be argued that it is unnecessary and undesirable to exclude small anti-democratic parties. That is a question of expediency only, and there is something to be said for the view that the tolerance even of such small parties or fractions tends to obscure the dangers threatened by attempts to establish dictatorships by constitutional methods. Faced by any such attempts, the democratic State is fully justified in excluding partisans of dictatorship from parliamentary representation, and in taking any ancillary measures. The advocates of dictatorship, repudiating all their democratic obligations, have no democratic rights. On the other hand, the democrats have a clear right to defend their institutions against any attack which goes beyond expression and dissemination of opinion. That may involve departure from normal democratic methods, but, in the circumstances, the requisite basis for democracy is destroyed or seriously weakened. The necessary degree of common agreement is lacking. Democrats do an ill service to their cause when they deny to democracy the right of self-defence. They make the same mistake as that which has led to such disastrous consequences in Germany.[1] It follows that democrats have the

[1] "Every imaginable thing was permitted in the German Republic, yet its form remains intact. But all the time its very elasticity was giving scope for the forces which were to destroy it. The tolerance to which the republic was pledged on principle was extended to cover attacks on its very existence."—Sieburg, *op. cit.* p. 273.

"It believed, for instance, that 'Democracy' implied that every single individual was to be allowed to engage in any activity whatever, even when this was directed against the structure of the

right to oppose by force any attempt to establish a dictatorship, even if it has majority support. The absurdity of the contention that the democrat is bound peacefully to acquiesce in a majority decision in favour of dictatorship is obvious, for once the dictatorship is established the chance of reversing the decision by a free majority vote has gone; the democratic method can no longer be utilised. Mr. Calvin B. Hoover has stated the position in the course of his study of the "Nazi" Revolution.

"For democracy to have a chance to succeed it is essential that there should be not only a majority but a very large majority of the people who are willing to accept it. This was to be proved in later years when a fifty-two per cent. majority of National Socialists and Nationalists was able to put an end to any future opportunity for the population to decide by a free vote, either who their political leaders were to be or what the system itself should be like. For democracy to endure, the democratic parties must never lose control; for one defeat at the polls is fatal, since once to lose control of the governmental apparatus is to lose the opportunity to submit again to the voters the question of whether or not there shall be a democratic form of government. This is the dilemma which confronts every democratic government

State, and thus it very soon became evident that the opponents of the Republic were receiving more advantage from her than were her closest and most faithful friends. . . . It would have been by no means undemocratic if all groups, grasping after dictatorship, had been excluded from the rights of Democracy, since to let them have their way would have amounted to an endangering of the rights of a far greater number of the people. The German Republic has never fully understood these things, and therein has been her undoing. It has almost seemed as though she felt it her duty to commit hara-kiri—as if this were also one of the rules of the democratic game."—Prince Hubertus Loewenstein, *The Tragedy of a Nation*, pp. 48–50.

and certainly justifies such governments in taking strong measures against parties or groups which proclaim their intention of using the ballot only as a means of destroying the democratic system."[1]

The present situation in this country does not, perhaps, warrant any such measures, but it is important that democrats should appreciate the need for determined action in the event of the problem threatening to become serious.

[1] *Germany Enters the Third Reich*, p. 41.

CONCLUSION

WE have attempted to state as clearly as possible the essentials of British parliamentary democracy, and the conditions upon which its continuance is dependent. Those conditions, in so far as they have been clarified, may appear to some minds all the more irksome. Indeed, they may possibly be regarded as unacceptable by some who might otherwise have been disposed to support parliamentary institutions. Communists and Fascists alike, undoubtedly, will find in these pages confirmatory evidence for their rejection of democratic methods. Nothing, however, is ever lost by clarification of the issues. If people do not wish to see a breakdown of our existing institutions, or to depart from our customary political methods, then it is all-important that they should realise what their maintenance involves. If they are unwilling to accept what is involved, then the sooner they are compelled to face up to the alternative or alternatives, the better it will be for all concerned. The democrat has nothing to fear, and much to gain, from the fullest and frankest discussion of the alternatives. The outcome of such discussion, we are confident, will be an increased admiration for the political system built up so slowly and arduously by our forbears and ourselves, a firmer determination not to endanger this the greatest of our national achievements, and a less grudging willingness to pay the price of patience, tolerance, moderation, concession, and acceptance of responsibility, which its retention entails. In our view, the benefits of peaceful orderly political development and of such political freedom as we now enjoy are well worth that price, and they should not be carelessly jeopardised or wantonly sacrificed.

Our feeling of pride in British parliamentary democracy is not diminished by our consciousness of its many imperfections. Whether the tests applied are those of humanity or of governmental efficiency, the defects of the system are of minor importance when contrasted with its merits and achievements, and comparison with other systems and methods, past or present, may be fearlessly challenged. Alike, in public spirit, in efficiency and honesty of administration, and in respect for human personality, this country has been, and still is, second to none. Whatever the shortcomings of the British people may be, it has not been found necessary to dragoon them into recognition of the supremacy of the public good. If, to many minds, political advance is ordinarily slow, it is relatively sure, and political life has, in fact, reached a higher stage of development here than elsewhere.

Decisions taken are effectively implemented, and, in times of crisis, whether of war or peace, our political machinery works with an expedition and efficiency to which autocracies seldom attain. Judged by results, British parliamentary democracy more than holds its own amongst the political systems known to mankind, even in those very respects in which authoritarian systems are so frequently alleged to be superior. These results, moreover, have not been attained at the expense of human dignity and freedom. On the contrary, they have been accompanied by a continuous extension both of the forms and the reality of voluntary political co-operation. Thus, not only are the advantages claimed for other methods secured as well or better by British methods, but to them are added the benefits of a wide measure of self-government. Moreover, the incompleteness of our political freedom, as has been pointed out, cannot legitimately be made an excuse for denial of the reality of that degree of political freedom we possess, still less for depriving us of it.

A balanced appreciation, of course, must give due weight to the need for adjustment and improvement, and pride in our political methods and institutions does not imply the slightest feeling of complacency. It would not be an easy task, under any circumstances, to conduct political life by the methods of democracy, and, in existing circumstances, the difficulties inherent in the democratic method are greatly complicated by the tangled problems which beset all systems of government in the post-war world. It may be urged that we have not paid sufficient attention to certain aspects of the present situation. We shall be reminded, no doubt, of the desirability of capable and energetic leadership in these difficult times. We do not for a moment dispute it, but such leadership is not always recognised, much less welcomed, when it is forthcoming; and we would point out to those who are dissatisfied that leaders of genius are not to be had for the asking, and that their rarity is not a feature peculiar to democracies. We may be told that unless sound policies are effectively pursued democratic government may perish. We agree; but that is also true of other systems of government. Moreover, there are always differences of opinion concerning both the soundness of policies proposed and the nature of their effects when applied.

We shall be reminded also of the congestion of business under parliamentary democracy. Here, again, we do not for a moment question the fact, nor have we any desire to make the evil appear less serious than it is. On the contrary, we assert that the problems arising from the rapid extension of the functions of the State and the limitations imposed by time and nature upon the powers of the individuals through whom the State must act are the major technical problems of government in the modern world. The sphere of governmental action is being continuously widened, while at the same time it is desired to maintain and strengthen unified direction and control. The inevitable result is a growing congestion of business at the centre, and a strain which threatens to become intolerable for the personnel of the political executive. These problems, however, are not peculiar to the democratic State. They are problems of government as such, and confront non-democratic States with almost equal force. Although their emergence has provided material for criticism of democratic methods, there is as yet no indication that countries employing other methods have met with a greater measure of success in dealing with them.

Congestion in Parliament itself constitutes, of course, an aspect of the problem from which non-parliamentary States are immune. However, congestion of business is not confined to legislatures. Indeed, it attains greater proportions in the sphere of executive action, and the difficulties there cannot be overcome by resort to the methods of dictatorship. In this matter, the only important advantages a dictatorship enjoys are that it is able to restrict the scope of discussion, to obscure the facts of the situation, and to override any opposition which may be forthcoming. Such advantages, we admit, may tempt those who are anxious to extend the activities of the State, but they leave the basic problems unsolved.

On whatever lines a way out of the dilemma may be sought, it is important to recognise that there are practical limits to effective State action, and that the roots of congestion of business are to be found not in faulty political machinery but in the increasing magnitude and complexity of the tasks which governments are being called upon to undertake.

In this country, of course, adjustments in the political machinery are continually being made in the traditional British manner, and, on the whole, what is required at the moment is further development on the lines indicated by the changes which have already taken place. The important thing, however, from the democratic standpoint, is to see that no adaptations are made at the cost of restricting profitable discussion. Indeed, from that standpoint, the aim should be to extend and improve the process of discussion.

We have given adequate evidence of a general disposition to improve as well as to preserve. We have noted, for instance, certain special defects in the political system, the most striking of which is the undemocratic constitution of the House of Lords. We have indicated, moreover, other and more important directions in which improvements are called for. Such improvements relate, for the most part, not to the political machinery, but to the spirit in which it is operated. The successful working of the British system depends upon recognition of the nature of democratic methods and greater practical conformity to them. It is not by formal changes that these things can be secured.[1] Responsibility rests upon the individual citizen, and upon the political parties and groups through which individuals seek to achieve their political objectives. Perhaps the greatest need at the present time is more effective co-operation in parties and between parties; and perhaps the greatest danger is the possible development of two major parties of extremists. Government cannot be conducted by democratic methods unless there is at least one party or combination of parties which maintains a broad basis and pursues a moderate and conciliatory policy. It is better that there should be two such bodies, but one is absolutely indispensable. That is the most urgent consideration which the supporter of democratic government has to bear in mind, whatever political opinions he or she may hold.

Up to the present, the British people have weathered the storm which has spread destruction throughout the world, and they have done so, not only without departure from democratic methods, but in no small measure because of adherence to them. By closer co-operation between parties, the perils of political instability and deadlock have been averted for a time, but the storm has not yet spent itself, and the dangers may recur. In the past, Great Britain has led the world

---

[1] Cessation of parliamentary obstruction, and renunciation of opposition either for the sake of opposition or for temporary partisan advantage, would do more, indeed, to facilitate the work of Parliament than any formal changes in procedure.

in the art of government; it has added to its laurels in the recent years of stress; and it is now the envy of lovers of freedom in many lands which have succumbed to the deceptive lure of violence and dictatorship. Not only in order to safeguard our own internal peace, liberty, and well-being, but as a hope and inspiration to others, we owe a vigilant and unwavering allegiance to the methods which have hitherto served us so well, and which have raised to so lofty a height our country's reputation.

PRINTED BY PURNELL AND SONS
PAULTON (SOMERSET) AND LONDON